Buy, Rent, and Sell

Buy, Rent, and Sell

How to Profit by Investing in Residential Real Estate

Robert Irwin

McGraw-Hill

New York   Chicago   San Francisco   Lisbon   London
Madrid   Mexico City   Milan   New Delhi   San Juan
Seoul   Singapore   Sydney   Toronto

Library of Congress Cataloging-in-Publication Data

Irwin, Robert, 1941-
    Buy, rent, and sell : a high profit strategy for real estate investing / Robert Irwin.
       p.   cm.
    ISBN 0-07-137337-3
    1. Real estate investment.   2. Real estate business. I. Title.
   HD1382.5.I689   2001
   332.63'24—dc21   00-069566

McGraw-Hill

A Division of The McGraw·Hill Companies

     5 6 7 8 9 0   AGM/AGM   0 9 8 7 6 5 4 3 2 1

ISBN 0-07-137337-3

It was set in Baskerville per the BSF TTS design by Joanne Morbit of the Professional Book Group's composition unit, Hightstown, N.J.

Printed and bound by Quebecor World/Martinsburg.

McGraw-Hill books are available at special quantity discounts to use as premiums and sales promotions, or for use in corporate training programs. For more information, please write to the Director of Special Sales, Professional Publishing, McGraw-Hill, Two Penn Plaza, New York, NY 10121-2298. Or contact your local bookstore.

This book contains the author's opinions. Some material in this book may be affected by changes in market conditions, or real estate law (or changes in interpretations of the law) since the manuscript was prepared. The accuracy and completeness of the information contained in this book cannot be guaranteed. Neither the author nor the publisher is engaged in rendering investment, legal, tax, accounting, or other similar professional services. If these services are required, the reader should obtain them from a competent professional.

For Janeth and David, who were the real inspiration for this book

Contents

Preface   ix

Part 1 Make Your Profit When You Buy

1. Where's the Profit?   3

2. Flip or Hold?   11

3. 10 Rules for Profiting from Real Estate Purchases   25

4. Making Lowball Offers That Get Accepted   39

5. Profit Strategy 1—Bargains from Motivated Sellers   47

6. Profit Strategy 2—Finding and Buying Foreclosures   53

7. Profit Strategy 3—Buying in Turnaround Areas   65

8. Profit Strategy 4—Working Lender-Owned Properties   71

9. Profit Strategy 5—Bargains in Government's Repos   85

10. Profit Strategy 6—Hidden Treasures in Handyman
    Specials   93

11. Profit Strategy 7—Finding Bargains on the Internet   103

12. Profit Strategy 8—Convert Your Old House
    to a Rental When You Move   111

Part 2 Multiply Your Cash

13. How to Get an Investment Mortgage   121

14. Unconventional Financing   129

Part 3 Renting in the Real World

15. Will It Make a Good Rental?   139

16. Irwin's 12 Rules for Successful Landlording   149

17. Turning an Alligator into a Cow   167

Part 4 Selling for Profit

18. Selling a Rental, Fast   179

19. Converting a Tenant to a Buyer   191

20. Dodging the Tax Bullet   203

21. The Real Estate Money Tree   217

    Appendix Why Inflation Is Your Friend   225

    Index   233

Preface

Back in 1991 when I wrote *Buy, Rent, and Hold,* I had no idea that it would be such a big seller. The book explained how to profit from the real estate recession that was occurring at that time. Apparently, a great many people successfully took the book's advice.

Today it's a different story. Today in most areas of the country it's no longer necessary to hold onto property for years and years to make a profit. Indeed, some inventive investors flip properties for huge profits in only a matter of days!

Thus, it was understandable that many requested a new book that would deal with today's new real estate market. *Buy, Rent, and Sell* is that new book. It offers a new approach to buying and selling real estate for profit. It shows how to use lender's money (instead of your own), which homes will make the most profit, which can be resold (flipped) for cash out, which should be held long term, and much more. This book is for today's market.

Don't sit on the sidelines and watch others profit from the best real estate market in decades. Get in and stake out your piece of the action. *Buy, Rent, and Sell* will show you how.

Robert Irwin

Part 1

Make Your Profit When You Buy

1
Where's the Profit?

Over the past five years, average people have gotten rich investing in small single-family and multiple-family rentals. They've bought houses and two-to-four-unit apartment buildings. A few have dabbled in small commercial buildings. Almost all of their returns over the five-year period have far exceeded their other investments, including IRAs, 401(k)s, and employer retirement plans. And they've done this with almost none of the down-side risks of stock investing.

Often these people began investing in realty not to become the neighborhood millionaire (although that happens more frequently than most people realize) but instead to pay for their children's college education, to lead a richer lifestyle, or to establish a nice nest egg for retirement. I was recently talking with a 68-year-old who told me, "Of all my investments over the years, the one that really paid off was the homes that I bought. Most of the 17 that I have are now free and clear, and they bring me over $11,000 a month in spendable income!"

On the same day I helped his son, who is 23, purchase his first rental property. He told me, "By the time I'm half dad's age, I plan to retire on my property holdings." I expect he will.

It seems that more people than ever understand the value of owning property since more people than at any other time in history own real estate in this country.

TIP

Most owners have watched the value of their homes skyrocket, and dream of their profits. The problem with that, of course, is that you always need a place to live, so if you sell and take your profits, you still need

another (usually more expensive) home to buy and
live in. As a result, some of these owners have realized
that the way to succeed is to buy second, third, or
even more homes. That way they can treat the other
properties as true investments and cash in on the
profits.

Why Is Real Estate a Hot Investment?

Of course, the appeal of real estate is the rapid price appreciation
seen in most parts of the country over the past five years. While 5 to
7 percent a year price appreciation has been common, price appreciation in some areas such as parts of Washington state, California,
Nevada, Texas, New York, and New England climbed at meteoric
rates sometimes 12 to 15 percent or more annually. One area,
Sacramento, California, recently saw a 22 percent price increase in
housing in just six months!

TRAP

When the market's hot, late night television bombards
you with real estate gurus. Every other show seems to
be, "How to Get Rich Quick in Real Estate." Anytime
anyone tells you that you can make piles of money
without working at it, without spending time or money,
without having skill or luck, watch out. Chances are
that person is trying to make his or her own fortune
out of your pocket!

Of course, real estate hasn't always gone up. Between 1990 and
1997 most parts of the country experienced a real estate recession
with prices falling as much as 30 percent over the entire period.
However, that was the first major recession in real estate since the
end of World War II, after 55 years of generally steady growth. And
the prospect for another long period of real estate growth from now
forward seems excellent.

Why Doesn't Real Estate Require a Lot of Money to Get Into?

If you were making 6 to 7 percent on your investment, you might consider it pretty good money. If you were making 20 percent, you'd probably be very happy. But, what if you were making 50 percent or more? How would you feel then?

You'd feel like those who invest in real estate.

It's all possible because of leverage. If you haven't seen how this works before, watch closely.

The amount you invest in a property is almost always leveraged. That means that you only have to put up a small amount of the purchase price, sometimes as little as only 3 percent down!

The result is that when prices go up, your percentage return is huge.

TIP

If you put 3 percent or $3,000 down on a $100,000 property and it goes up 3 percent in value, you've doubled your money: you've made 100 percent! (A 3 percent increase moves the price up $3,000.)

TRAP

Of course, in real life it's not quite that simple. There are the costs of purchase and, ultimately, the costs of sale. As a result, you really get the big return in the second year of ownership. Some of the first year's appreciation goes toward offsetting transaction costs.

Leveraging—Annual Return on 10 Percent Down

Price Appreciation	Your Return
3%	30%
4	40
5	50
6	60

(Continued)

Leveraging—Annual Return on 10 Percent Down (*Continued*)

Price Appreciation	Your Return
7	70
8	80
9	90
10	100
11	110
12	120
13	130
14	140
15	150
16	160
17	170
18	180
19	190
20	200%!

What Makes This Possible?

It's all possible because in recent years lenders, facing stiff competition for mortgage dollars, have reduced the amount of down payment required to purchase an investment property. In the past the minimum down payment was as high as 30 percent of the purchase price, and certainly no less than 20 percent. However, in recent years lenders have lowered the rail until now it's common to buy an investment house with only 10 percent down. (If you buy the house with plans to live in it, your down payment can be as low as the 3 percent noted above.)

Even if you put 10 percent down on a property and it appreciates 10 percent, you've still made 100 percent on your investment! But if it goes up 20 percent, your return on investment is 200 percent!

Flipping

Of course, as price appreciation goes higher and higher, the market tends to get frantic. Usually it means that there is a shortage of homes, with buyers competing. That results in the increase of a different kind of phenomenon commonly called "flipping."

Here, buyers don't bother to hold and rent the properties they buy. Rather, they quickly resell them, sometimes during escrow, for a higher price. Thus, it may be possible to flip a property and quickly make a significant profit, between $10,000 and $100,000. This yields the money needed to invest in more properties.

Flipping, however, has some serious downside risks including potential legal concerns. We'll look more closely at flipping in the next chapter.

Renting

The key to successful long-term real estate investing is renting the property for your annual costs (or close to them). If you can do that, then the property essentially pays for itself (after the down payment and closing costs). Each year you hold it, its value goes up. In a sense it can become the perfect investment—going up in price, yet not costing money to maintain. Many investors see property as a long-term investment, five years or more. Of course, at any time you may be able to refinance to get some of your money out. We'll examine this strategy in the last chapter.

In years past, however, it was difficult to find properties that could yield a high enough rental return to pay for the "nut" that the investors had. This was typically referred to as "PITI" or Principal, Interest, Taxes, and Insurance.

TRAP

Many novice investors overlook maintenance and vacancy expense, which can run as high as 15 or 20 percent of the total rental income annually.

In the past investors would make the mistake of buying "alligators." These were properties where the expenses far and away exceeded the rental income. As a result, the investor was required to dip into his or her own pocket to make up the monthly difference. These unlucky investors would often say that their properties were "eating me alive!" Hence, they became known in the trade as alligators.

Depending on your tax bracket and a few other factors, you may be able to deduct depreciation and other expenses on your rental property from your ordinary income. We'll discuss this in more detail in Part 4.

Over the past few years, however, a housing shortage has changed things. A lack of suitable housing in many areas has driven rental prices up. And now, for the first time in decades, it is possible for investors to make their nut with their rental income.

Will Rogers once said that the thing about real estate is that, "They ain't makin' any more of it." As this is proven by housing shortages in many areas of the country (particularly California and parts of the West), real estate has become an ever better investment.

What About Landlording?

Of course, to get a steady flow of income from your property, you must have good tenants. I've been a landlord for more years than I care to remember, and I can honestly say that except for one or two bad apples, almost all of my tenants were wonderful people. They paid their rent on time, they maintained my property well, and they left under amicable conditions. Most landlords I've talked with have had similar experiences.

However, that doesn't mean, as I've indicated, that you can't get a bad apple in the bunch. One bad tenant can create a lot of headaches. All of which is to say that if you're going to become a real estate investor, you had better learn to be a good landlord. We'll look into how to do this in Part 3.

What About Ease of Selling?

Finally, there's the matter of getting your money out at the end of the road—collecting your profits. There are loads of opportunities here.

You may want to simply sell all or part of your rental investments and take your money in cash. The profit can be substantial. As I write this book, I am looking at associates who are currently selling property they bought less than four years ago and profiting $100,000 or more *per house*! One is selling a small (three-unit) apartment building for nearly double what she paid!

You can join the winner's circle, too. The biggest complaint I've heard from sellers is the size of the the taxes they have to pay on their profits. (Wouldn't that be a wonderful situation to have?!) We'll discuss ways of dodging the tax bullet in Chapter 20.

Can I Refi Cash Out?

Finally, as suggested earlier, there's the tried and true method of refinancing to get your cash out. You buy the property and then instead of selling, you refinance to get your money out. If you're judicious, you can carry this on indefinitely, your real estate supplying you with replenished wealth. We'll see exactly how to do this in Chapter 21.

And there you have it—a road map for success in real estate in the twenty-first century. Most people already have most of what they need to succeed. In many cases all that's required is that you learn and then apply yourself. Of course, you also do need a good real estate market. But the United States is happy to supply that for you.

2
Flip or Hold

How do you want to make your money in real estate? Do you want quick returns? Or would you prefer the solid security of long-term income and growth?

You can have both!

In a hot market, flipping is the fastest way to make money. This simply means that you gain control of a piece of property and lock in the price, and then you "flip it." You sell it to someone else at a higher price. And you profit the difference. In a strong or even a colder market, holding makes more sense. (We'll see the advantages of holding instead of flipping later in this chapter.)

How Do I Flip a Property?

Let's say you purchase a property for $30,000 below market price. (We'll see how to do this in the next 10 chapters.) Your price is $100,000. However, instead of actually buying it, you just tie it up, thereby locking in the price. Then you quickly bring in a buyer who pays full market price—$130,000. You pocket the difference, less any minor costs of the transaction. (For our purposes, "flipping" means controlling a property, not actually completing a purchase and then a sale. If your goal is to actually purchase a property and hold it for awhile—even just a few months—see the next section on holding.)

TIP

"Market Price" means what the property will bring on the open market, given enough time and adequate exposure to buyers.

Can this really be done? Yes, it's done all the time, particularly when the market is hot. Here are the five rules for flipping:

Rules for Flipping

1. **Buy right**—You can only flip if you buy below market price.
2. **Lock in a price**—If the seller can get out of the deal, he or she may try to get the higher resale price themselves.
3. **Don't take title**—You don't want to own the property; the transaction costs will kill you.
4. **Have a buyer waiting in the wings**—These are fast deals, so you don't have time to go looking for a buyer.
5. **Provide full disclosure**—The way to avoid trouble in these deals is to make sure everyone knows everything. (We'll have more to say about this shortly.)

Do Investors Really Flip Properties?

Have you ever seen lines of people waiting outside the sales office when new homes go up for sale?

This happens when the market is hot and there are shortages of homes. Do you think that all of those people are waiting in line to buy a home to live in? If you do, you would be mistaken.

Many of those people are hoping to flip the property. If there are 20 new homes being built and the demand is for 500 (as has been the case in some areas over recent years), that means that 480 people are not going to get a NEW home. If you're one of the lucky 20, you can quickly sell to one of the unlucky others.

TIP

In some lineups for new homes, people will even sell a good place in line (if it's close to the front) for hundreds or thousands of dollars! To avoid this practice (remember, the builders want all the profit), some builders have taken to getting the names of people in line. However, it's usually easy enough to say that the person who's name is on the list was simply a place-holder for the new buyer who takes his or her place.

In a hot market, flipping also takes place in resales. Savvy investors locate properties that are for sale at below market, tie them up, and then quickly resell. Sometimes the sales are from foreclosures, REOs, probates, or just from sellers who want out quickly and are willing to take less. (Again, check the next chapters for how to locate such properties.)

Can I Flip in a Cold Market?

When the market slows down, it's harder to flip. On the one hand, it's much easier to find bargain properties. However, on the other it's harder to find rebuyers (the next buyers who purchase through you) who are willing to move quickly. The reason is that when the market slows down, buyers become more cautious. They want to see that they are getting a bargain. Therefore, in order to flip, you have to reduce your profit and give the buyer a good reason to purchase quickly . . . or wait until the market heats up again.

TRAP

Remember, in any market, you must buy a property below market value in order to flip. If you buy at market, you will have to hold onto the property until it goes up before you can resell. Beware of trying to sell for more than market value. You won't succeed, except when the market's red hot and there are multiple offers on every property.

How Do I Actually Flip a Property?

The mechanics of the deal are fairly straightforward. Once you locate a property that's below market, you present your offer. If the seller accepts, you have a period of time in which to resell. Depending on how that offer was structured, your time period can be anywhere from a minimum of about 30 days to a maximum of about 6 months.

You then bring in a rebuyer (one who actually purchases the property) who concludes the sale with the original seller. The cash transfer is done in escrow. The new buyer gets a mortgage and puts up a cash down payment in the usual fashion. A portion of the purchase price goes to cash out the original seller. And you get the remainder, usually in cash, but sometimes in the form of a second mortgage, for yourself.

In the transaction noted at the beginning of this chapter, the rebuyer pays $130,000 in the form of a down payment and a new mortgage. (The rebuyer may only be putting up as little 3 percent down—that can make it an excellent deal for him or her!)

The escrow pays the seller the $100,000 in cash that you locked in as your price. And you get the difference, roughly $30,000, less a few transaction costs.

How Do I Lock In the Seller's Price Without Actually Buying the Property?

There are two methods, assignment and option. The one I prefer is the option.

What's a Real Estate Option?

A real estate option is quite straightforward. A real estate option is, in reality, not much different from a stock option. For the buyer, it is an opportunity (but not a requirement) to purchase for a set price by some future date. For the seller it is a commitment to sell for a set price by a set date.

How a Real Estate Option Works

1. You locate the property and make an option offer.
2. If the seller accepts, you give the sellers some option money. They give you the option to buy the property at a fixed price for a certain amount of time.

3. You later exercise your option by buying the property, or in our case, by selling your option to a rebuyer for a profit.

Note that in an option, you the buyer are *not* committed to purchase. It's at your discretion. The seller, however, is committed to sell. He or she must go through with the transaction, IF you execute your option.

Why would a seller agree to such a thing? Cash!

As noted, in order to get an option, you pay the seller some money. It can be any amount, but it has to be enough to persuade him or her to give you an option. A typical amount might be between $500 and $5,000, depending on the value of the property.

The term of the option is likewise negotiable. Usually it runs from 30 days to 6 months, but it can be longer or shorter.

Let's take an example: You find a property that is $30,000 below market. Instead of buying it, you give the seller $1,000 for an option to buy the property for $100,000 anytime during the next three months. Now, you've locked in the price and the property.

Next, you find a buyer to purchase the property at $130,000. You have about two months (plus a month to close) to accomplish this. (See the last section of this book for tips on finding buyers fast.)

Once you find your buyer, you sell that person the property. Escrow is opened and, as part of the process, your option is exercised. The rebuyer purchases the property, which you technically buy from the seller by using your option. As a practical matter, the rebuyer gets a new mortgage and puts up a down payment, the seller gets his or her price as defined by the option agreement, and you get the difference, in the case of our example, $30,000.

What Are the Plusses of the Option?

- You've tied up the property at a fixed price.
- You don't have to qualify for nor obtain a mortgage. You also don't have to come up with a down payment.
- You have time to find a buyer, as long as six months or more.
- You don't own the property, so you're not responsible for mortgage payments, taxes, insurance, maintenance, or repairs.
- You've got a relatively small amount of cash tied up.

What Are the Minuses of the Option?

- You have to put up some money. (Obviously, as little as possible!) The seller gets this money and keeps it. Depending on how the option is written, it may be deducted from the sales price to you when and if you exercise your option.
- If you don't exercise your option before it expires, you lose your option money (the amount you put up).
- If property values go down during the option period, you'll have trouble finding a buyer.
- The seller may want a quick sale and refuse to give you an option.

I've given and taken options on real estate. They can work for both buyers and sellers. As a buyer, we've seen some obvious advantages such as tying up the property for a small amount of money and giving you time to locate a rebuyer and conclude a sale. For a seller, they provide either income (the option money) or a sale.

In What Situation Wouldn't I Be Able to Use an Option?

The biggest problem with options, as far as I'm concerned, is that most sellers willing to sell below market want a quick, not a delayed sale. They may be facing foreclosure, or other financial problems. There could be a divorce or a death in the family. In all such cases, they may need to get cash now. Your offer of an option may be appealing, but it won't cut the mustard if they need to be out of the property within 30 days (which, indeed, may be the compelling reason they are willing to sell for a low price).

For more information on the lease-option, check into Chapter 19.

If you can't get an option, the other way to tie up the property without buying it is to use an assignment of purchase. This is just a tiny bit trickier.

How Do I Assign My Purchase?

You make an offer to purchase. However, when you make your offer, you write your name and then "or assigns." What this means is that either you can buy the property, or whomever else you assign the contract to can buy the property. (First-timers should have an attorney handle the language appropriate for your state.)

TRAP

Savvy sellers won't always agree to an "or assigns" sales contract. The reason is that they don't know who will eventually purchase the property. They are afraid that you might not be able to get a needed mortgage and want a back door out, or that you're planning to sell your contract to someone else (which is, in fact, the case!) and that person may not qualify for a needed mortgage. In order to calm the seller's fears, you may need to put up a bigger deposit, or avoid putting many escape clauses into the contract, which can increase your risks.

Unlike the option, the assignment runs for as long as a normal closing, typically 30 to 45 days. That means that you've got to find a buyer and conclude your other end of the deal very quickly.

Hopefully you have done your homework and have a rebuyer waiting in the wings, but of course for a higher price. When the deal is ready to close, the rebuyer's name, not yours, is placed on the deed.

Again, you never actually make the purchase. The transaction is basically handled in escrow. At the end of the deal, you get your money out, typically in cash.

Plusses of Assigning the Purchase

- Little cash involved—You only have to put up the original deposit when you buy the property from the seller, and you get this back from your rebuyer.
- Quick deal—You can expect to get your profit out within 30 to 45 days.
- You don't have to qualify for or obtain a mortgage.
- You don't own the property, so you're not responsible for mortgage payments, taxes, insurance, maintenance, or repairs.

Minuses of Assigning the Purchase

- You actually do commit to purchasing the property. To protect yourself from having to complete the purchase in case you can't find a buyer (or your buyer falls through), you'll want lots of escape clauses. But escape clauses weaken your offer and lessen your chances of getting it accepted. So to make the deal, you may have to take a big risk.

- If not handled properly, you can make the buyer or seller seriously mad at you, and you can land yourself in a lawsuit.

- The seller may not be able to complete the sale for any number of reasons, so you'll again need lots of escape clauses to protect yourself from the rebuyer. Again, such clauses weaken your sales agreement.

Does an Assignment Really Work?

Certainly it does. It's been used in real estate for as long as I can remember, and my memory goes back a long ways. However, as noted above, you need to include lots of escape clauses in the deal in case you can't find a buyer in the short amount of time that you have, or in case that buyer for some reason can't complete the purchase.

Escape clause? What's that?

It's very commonly used in most real estate sales transactions. It's a clause that says the sale/purchase is "subject to" or "contingent upon" something. If that something happens, you can gracefully (without financial harm) back out of the deal. In modern transactions there are three widely accepted escape clauses that most sellers will agree to without blinking (and that won't weaken the transaction). These are considered below.

Escape Clauses That Can Let You Get Out of the Deal

1. **Finance contingency**—You have written into the contract that the deal is contingent upon your getting financing. No financing, no deal and you're out without penalty. This usually runs for 30 days, but you must reasonably look for financing.

2. **Disclosure contingency**—You must approve the seller's disclosures. If you don't approve them, there's no deal. But the time limit here is very short. In California, for example, it's three days by law.

3. **Professional inspection**—You must approve a professional inspector's report. If you don't approve it, there's no deal. Usually you have 14 days to get the report and then either approve or disapprove it.

The problem with these contingencies is that they probably don't offer you enough protection if you're doing an assignment. For example, in order to get the deal at a cut-rate price, you may have to offer the seller cash. In a cash sale, you don't have the protection of a finance contingency.

You might rely on the disclosure and professional inspection contingency, but those usually run out after 14 days max. At that time you either agree to move forward without their protection, or back out of the deal. If you agree to move forward, and something adverse happens (for example, your rebuyer peters out), you're stuck for the house!

What About Other Contingencies?

As a result, most investors who are flipping using an assignment want to add other contingencies. These are easy to add, but not easy to get accepted.

You can make the sale contingent on anything: your uncle dying and giving you an inheritance, your great aunt coming from Australia to approve the deal, sun spots, anything at all. However, any contingency you add that's not reasonable (such as those three mentioned above) is likely to be considered frivolous by the seller and a reason not to sell to you. Thus, the more escape clauses to protect yourself that you include, the less likely you are to get the seller to sign. And the fewer escape clauses you include, the greater your risk in case you can't get a rebuyer to close the deal.

Isn't There Some Way to Limit My Liability Here?

There may be a way to limit your liability in case you can't make the deal. Most modern purchase agreements include a "liquidated damages" clause. If you sign this (and the seller does, too), then the total amount of damages that you are likely to have to pay in the event you don't (or can't) make the deal, is limited to your deposit. If you only put up a $1,000 deposit, you don't have a great deal at risk.

TRAP

Don't rely entirely on the liquidated damages clause. A nasty seller can hire an attorney to challenge it and you could spend a lot more money defending yourself in court.

Some readers, I'm sure, are asking why are all these cautions necessary for an assignment.

The reason is that assigned purchase agreements tend to be rather iffy. There's a lot that can go astray between signing them and actually concluding a sale between seller and rebuyer. If the sale can't be concluded, the seller is, of course, likely to get angry. And you want some good cover when that happens.

What's the Dirty Little Secret of Assignment Flipping?

There's an inherent problem in using an assignment to flip a property. Unfortunately, I've yet to see midnight gurus (some of those who promote it on late night television and elsewhere) explain this. So here goes.

Almost all sellers have a kind of personal relationship with their buyer. They want to know who's buying their property. (This is even the case with banks, which almost always insist on knowing exactly with whom they're dealing.) When you assign the purchase agreement, you break that bond. Most buyer and sellers, nevertheless, are willing to go along provided the deal concludes in a reasonable fashion. After all, they're still getting a purchase or a sale out of it.

However, when they discover that you're reselling the property at a substantial profit, some are very unhappy. After all, they conclude, what are you adding to the deal? They feel that your profit should go into their pocket.

TIP

Don't expect sellers to recognize the fact that, for whatever reason, they themselves couldn't get full market price for the property. (If they could've, they would've.) What you're bringing to the transaction is your marketing expertise.

As a result, you could have an angry seller (or buyer) on your hands who at the least refuses to sign off on the deal unless he or she gets more money, or at the worst, takes you to court. Thus, to oil the waters, many investors who flip in this manner just don't tell the buyer or seller. What they don't know won't hurt them.

Therein lies the rub. There shouldn't be anything illegal or even unethical in flipping property, *as long as all parties involved are made aware of what's happening.* However, when one party doesn't know what's going on, there are all kinds of opportunity for things to go wrong.

If they're being frank, any good investor will tell you that flipping works best in secret. If the seller doesn't realize you're making a $30,000 profit on the sale, he or she isn't likely to complain. But, in the same breath that good investor will tell you to bite the bullet and let the seller know. It will save you all sorts of trouble later on.

Remember, it shouldn't make any difference what you do with property after you and the seller agree on price and terms. If you can flip it to another buyer for a better price, so be it.

Will the Rebuyer Get Mad at Me?

Probably not, if you handle it wisely by letting the buyer know what you're paying for the property (and getting confirmation on a signed statement from the buyer). On the other hand, if you conceal the information, the buyer may discover it later on and think you were trying to pull a fast one, and go after you.

TIP

Surprisingly, as long as you're selling at market, most rebuyers won't care in the least that you're flipping or how much you're making on the deal. As long as they're assured they aren't paying too much, chances are they'll be happy.

Beware of Using Double Escrows

A double escrow is designed to deceive a buyer and a seller. It's where there are two escrows held simultaneously. In one you are the buyer and in the other you are the seller. They close simultaneously—you buy the property from the seller in one and simultaneously sell it to the rebuyer in the other. In a double escrow, which can go by several different names, only you know what's going on. The seller only deals with you in one escrow and the rebuyer only deals with you in the other. They never deal with each other and, hence, don't have direct knowledge of the total deal.

It is most certainly illegal for a real estate agent to conduct a double escrow and receive an undisclosed profit from a property he or she is listing. It should be illegal or unethical for an investor to do the same thing. The simple, sure way to avoid problems is to avoid double escrowing a property.

What's the Right Way?

The right way to handle a flip is to be sure that all parties know what you're doing (and get it in writing in case someone should later have an attack of memory failure). Quite often when they learn of it, they'll admire you for it. After all, remember that you're providing a sale for a seller who wants to get out. And you're providing a home for a buyer who wants to get in. Why shouldn't you be entitled to a profit for that? It's a win, win, win situation! (Remember, first-timers should get an attorney to help with an assignment.)

Take Paper As Your Profit

Thus far we've been speaking of getting your money out as cash. However, oftentimes it's hard to find a buyer who can come up with sufficient credit to get an almost 100 percent mortgage, or who can come up with sufficient cash for a big down payment to a lesser mortgage. Therefore, you may find that it's to your advantage to get a second mortgage on a flip.

This works in the same ways as described above for options and assignments. Except that when it's time for you to get your money out of the deal, there isn't enough cash to make it happen. So you give the rebuyer a second mortgage. You then get paid so much a month until you get all your money back, which usually happens a few years down the road when the rebuyer sells the property once again. (Alternatively, you could sell your second mortgage at a discount for cash. In the early years of the mortgage, however, expect the discount to be very heavy, as much as 50 percent, because the buyer of the mortgage assumes the risk that the rebuyer of the property won't keep making the payments.)

TIP

Be sure your second mortgage has an alienation clause in it. This means when the rebuyer sells, your mortgage must be paid off. It cannot be assumed by the next buyer. This can easily be inserted by any escrow company.

Of course, it goes without saying that you would want your rebuyer to be a good credit risk, or else you wouldn't get all of your money out of the second mortgage. Many investors "age" these second mortgages for six months to a year before selling them for cash. Aged mortgages have a much smaller discount.

Watch Out for Mortgage, Appraisal, or Buyer Manipulation

What's given flipping a bad name more than anything else over the past few years are unscrupulous investors who have manipulated mortgages, appraisals, and buyers. Rather than do the real work of the transaction, namely finding properties that are selling below market, they have purchased properties at actual market and then, through manipulation, sold them for above market to unwary buyers. This has been done in apparent collusion with lenders who secured higher appraisals than were warranted and made bigger loans than were justified. Often these properties were sold to poor minority rebuyers who really didn't understand about market value or how high their payments would be. Subsequently, when these rebuyers couldn't make stiff payments, the houses were lost to foreclosure.

That's where the real trouble started for these unscrupulous flippers. Almost all home mortgages are in one way or another insured or guaranteed through the government or a government-related agency (FHA, VA, Fannie Mae, Freddie Mac, and so forth). When the government began taking these properties back, it found out what was happening, and launched criminal investigations into the flippers.

This is not something you ever want to have happen to you. Always do the right thing: find undervalued properties. There are plenty of them out there to go around. Then, let everyone know what's happening in the deal, and get legitimate loans and appraisals. You'll do the seller, the rebuyer, the government, and even yourself a big favor.

What About Holding the Property?

The other side of the coin is to buy and then hold, waiting for prices to go up so that you can later resell for a big profit. Buying and holding is how most real estate millionaires made their money.

TIP

There are many real estate investors who own dozens, sometimes hundreds of properties, having accumulated them over the years. Their fortunes are solid as the Rock of Gibraltar. People always have to have a place to live, and there will always be rent to collect.

The key to holding property over time is to buy right. You need to structure your financing so that you can afford to make the payments from the rent generated. And you need to be able to rent out the property without hassle and then be able resell it. That means recognizing a home that's easily rented for good money and then easily resold. We'll go into detail in how to find these properties in the next chapters in this part and then also in the third part of this book.

Some people, however, aim to buy and hold for just a short time—three to six months—then resell. The trick here is to minimize the holding costs. These include the transaction fees (title insurance, escrow, commission, and so on) and the mortgage fees (points and assorted loan charges). Check into Part 2 for ways to minimize your costs.

Should I Flip or Hold?

Sometimes you'll have the option. (What a wonderful position to be in!) What should you do?

The answer is that whenever you can flip a property, do it. Don't hang onto the property.

The reason is simple. For every flippable property you find, you'll find half a dozen or more perfectly acceptable properties that you can hold. Finding holders is easy; finding flippers is hard.

Further, you need the cash that flipping can generate. Holding properties tends to drain cash away. Often there is some small negative cash flow. And it can take years before you can get cash out of the holders in order to buy more properties. (See ways to do it in Chapter 21.)

There's really no big decision here. If you can generate cash from a flippable property, go for it. You can always find a holder tomorrow.

3

10 Rules for Profiting from Real Estate Purchases

One of the oldest rules in real estate is that you make your money when you buy, not when you sell. Buy right and you'll always be able to rent the property out and eventually resell for good money. Buy wrong, and the property will be an alligator (it will eat you alive with payments) and give you trouble selling. Here are my 10 rules for making money when you buy a property.

10 Rules for Profit from Real Estate

RULE # 1—BUY SINGLE (OR SMALL MULTIFAMILY) HOUSING

RULE # 2—LOOK IN BETTER (BUT NOT THE BEST) NEIGHBORHOODS

RULE # 3—LOOK FOR FLIPPABLE PROPERTIES (WHERE YOU CAN CASH OUT)

RULE # 4—LOOK FOR STRONG TENANT MARKETS

RULE # 5—ONLY BUY PROPERTY WITH A GOOD PRICE/RENT RATIO

RULE # 6—KNOW WHAT YOUR REAL EXPENSES WILL BE

RULE # 7—GO FOR FAVORABLE TERMS

RULE # 8—GET A BARGAIN PRICE, NOT AN INFLATED VALUE

RULE # 9—ALWAYS LOWBALL THE SELLER

RULE # 10—NEVER BUY FAR FROM HOME

Let's consider each separately.

Rule #1—Buy Single (or Small Multifamily) Housing

I like houses best. The reason is simple: they are easy to buy (financing is readily available). They are easy to rent (most people prefer them to any other type of housing). They are comparatively easy to maintain. And when it comes time to resell, you get the highest profits.

Don't listen to so-called professional investors who knock the single-family home as an investment. I have heard those who can afford to buy 100-unit apartment buildings disparage the house. They might say, "If I have a 100-unit building and I have one vacancy, it's only 1 percent of my income that I'm losing. But if you have a single-family house and have one vacancy, you lose 100 percent of your income. There's no way to justify that!"

Baloney! If you have one unit and find one tenant, you have 100 percent occupancy. If you have a 100-unit apartment, you have to find 100 tenants to get full occupancy.

Either way, it's just a war of words. What counts are results. I've been renting single-family housing for more than 20 years in good markets and bad, and as long as I've been doing it personally, I've never had serious trouble finding a tenant. And I've always sold for a profit. My feeling is that if you're new to investment real estate, the best place to start is with a single-family house.

Condos: As a general rule, beware of condos as an investment. The temptation to buy may prove nearly irresistible, since they are typically offered at lower prices than houses. Historically, however, condos perform poorly. In a down market they fall first in value and go lower. In an up market, they are the last to rebound and their price increases tend to be the slowest. Further, condos will often rent for only 70 to 80 percent of the rate of a comparably sized single-family home. It may seem very appealing to buy a lower-cost condo, but you'll find them harder to rent and harder to sell.

TIP

Don't overlook the "hidden costs" of condominium ownership, mainly home owner's association (HOA) fees. These can often add hundreds of dollars a month to your payments.

Duplexes, Triplexes, Flats, Etc.: These often make good investments especially if they are located in an area of mainly single-family homes. You can sometimes buy them relatively cheaply (when compared to single-family homes) and rent them for most, if not all, of your payment. Upon resale, they tend to hold up well. Best of all, unlike condos, they tend to have no HOA fees.

TRAP

Beware of trying to combine home and investment here. Many people buy a duplex or triplex thinking to rent out one or two units to help offset costs while living in the remaining unit. The thought is that you have both a home and an investment property. The reality is that you end up with the worst of both possible worlds. You don't really have a home because your tenant is right next door. (He or she will be over every other minute with complaints.) In addition you don't really have a good rental because you're not able to offer a single-family detached home that can command top dollar.

Co-ops: These are great to live in, but impossible rentals. The Board will be on your back all the time if you try to rent out the property. They may want to approve every tenant, holding up the rental process. Additionally, some co-ops may try to restrict your ability to rent your property at all.

Small Apartment Buildings: These are a mixed bag for the investor. Mainly it's a matter of management. You will find that you have far more tenant movement here. If you have four houses, chances are you might change only one or two tenants during a year. With a four-unit apartment building, you might change as many as four or more tenants during that same time frame! Managing an apartment building is double or triple the work of managing the same number of single-family housing units.

TIP

My suggestion is that until you've handled a few rental houses, hold up on tackling even a small apartment building.

On the other hand, profits upon selling can be enormous. The value of apartment buildings is directly related to their rental income. The higher the rental income, the greater the value. The surest way to make money in real estate is to buy an apartment building, jack up the rents, and then resell. Typically for each dollar you increase your annual rental income you could get between six and twelve dollars in profit on the sale. If you have four units and raise the rent twenty-five dollars on each, that means an extra $100 a month or $1,200 a year. Multiply this times a multiple of, for example, 10, and you've got an instant profit of $12,000—all on a modest $25 a month rent increase! (Beware, however, of rent control areas where it is impossible to increase rental rates.)

Rule #2—Look in Better (but Not the Best) Neighborhoods

The better the neighborhood, the easier it will be to rent and eventually to sell (or trade) your property. Homes in good neighborhoods are always in demand, while those in poor neighborhoods languish. On the other hand, don't try for the very best areas. They are often over-priced and you'll find it hard to find an investment property there that will rent for enough to cover your monthly costs.

Homes in the top neighborhoods, however, often make the best flip properties. If you buy low here, you often have the best chance to immediately resell for a big profit.

What makes a good neighborhood? Look for attractive homes; and avoid areas where landscaping is neglected. Look for wide streets; avoid areas where abandoned cars litter streets. Look for conformity in housing; avoid areas where there is a hodgepodge of homes.

TIP

Check the schools. The biggest indicator of a good neighborhood is that it has quality schools, as evidenced by high scores on standardized tests (always available at the main school district office, or online). Poor schools mean a poor neighborhood.

Rule #3—Look for Flippable Properties

The term "flipping" has come into the real estate vernacular along with the big boom in property values. It essentially means that you quickly buy and then resell a property without holding on to it for long. If you can flip a property and can make cash on it, the reasoning goes, do it.

I agree, up to a point. The cash generated by flipping can go toward your own income (supporting yourself) as well as toward creating capital for the down payment on another property. Flipping, when possible, has always been a good way to generate cash from real estate.

The mistake that some people make, however, is to look *only* for flippable properties, or to try and flip properties that really aren't suitable. It makes little sense to flip a property to make $10,000 when if you hold it for a year you, can make $100,000. Also, out of 10 properties you look at, you'll be lucky to find one that's truly flippable. Yet, five of the others might be good for holding, renting, and then reselling.

TIP

Building long-term wealth involves holding and renting a majority of your real estate.

Check back to the last chapter for more on flipping.

Rule #4—Look for Strong Tenant Markets

It's a truism that there are always tenants. But, the underlying fact is that in some locales, there are more tenants than in others. And in some locales, the tenant population can afford to pay a higher rent than in others. Ideally, you want to buy in an area where there are lots of high-income tenants.

It's important, here, to think locally. The country may be doing well economically, but your area may be doing better, or worse, than the nation as a whole. In order to get a tenant for your property, you must be able to draw on local workers. If there are few well-paying local jobs, you won't get many good tenants.

As a consequence, it's important to do a tenant analysis before leaping ahead and buying rental property. There are a variety of ways to accomplish this: First, if you're buying into low-income housing, look for blue-collar tenants. That means industrial plants will be nearby. On the other hand, if you're buying an upscale property, look for white-collar workers. Check in the area for office buildings, commercial buildings, financial institutions, and the like.

Second, think like a tenant. If you're a tenant, who's going to employ you? Look around the area. Who are the big employers? Find the place that the tenant wants to live and that's where you'll have your strongest tenant market.

Third, check the local newspapers under "Homes for Rent." You'll quickly see which areas have rentals. Call to see what the prices are (if they aren't listed). Then recheck the same paper over several weeks. If you find areas which have the same homes advertised for weeks on end, avoid those. If there are areas where homes rarely crop up and then the ad appears only for a single weekend, go there. That's where the tenants want to live! Areas which rent quickly indicate a good rental market. Areas with lots of vacancies do not.

Finally, check with brokers and rental agencies. Often in a single conversation they can give you as much information as you could collect in weeks of conducting your own investigations. (It's a good idea to do some personal leg work anyway, just to be sure that what you are being told is, in fact, accurate.)

Rule #5—Only Buy Property with a Good Price/Rent Ratio

Your strategy is to mostly buy and rent out property until you can sell for a hefty profit. But in order to hold that property, you have to be able to rent it for enough money to pay your expenses.

Can you realistically do that? Can you find rental property that will cover all your expenses? In truth, it sometimes can be difficult. However, it's not impossible, particularly after taking into consideration tax benefits of ownership.

However, observing the rule that you should look before leaping, I always check the price/rent ratio on any property BEFORE buying it. That way I avoid surprises. Some properties seem like they should be able to carry themselves, or close to it, but upon analysis reveal that they are instead alligators. If you buy without checking this ratio, you're at risk.

The price/rent ratio is simply a rule of thumb that wise investors use to gauge the relationship between monthly rental income, monthly expenses, and the price of the property. It simply says that the monthly income from rents should be around 1 percent of the total purchase price. If the monthly rent is less than 1 percent, unless the property is flippable, that property might be just too expensive. Here's how to make the calculation:

$$\text{RATIO} = \frac{\text{PURCHASE PRICE}}{\text{MONTHLY RENT}}$$

If your property has a value of $200,000 then 1 percent is simply $2,000. If it can't generate around $2,000 in rent, you probably won't be able to cover your monthly payments. If your property's value is $500,000, it should be able to generate around $5,000. This would result in your having to take money (possibly a lot of money) out of your own pocket each month just to hang onto the property. No one wants to do that, certainly not for any extended period of time.

TIP

The ratio is just a "rule of thumb" and depends heavily on the interest rate of your mortgage. If rates are down around 7 percent or lower, then adjust the price/rent ratio to ¾. If they are 10 percent or higher, adjust the rate to around 1¼.

With a really bad ratio, you're probably better off passing on the property, even if otherwise it seems like a good deal.

Rule #6—Know What Your Expenses Will Be

If knowing your true rental income is important, knowing your true rental expenses can be even more important. You can't know whether the property will float until and unless you know both.

Typical Basic Rental Expenses
PITI (Principle, Interest, Taxes, Insurance)

Mortgage payments (Principal and Interest)

Taxes

Insurance

These are the easiest to determine. Just contact a mortgage broker to find the PITI. Give him or her the amount of your mortgage and you'll quickly get the monthly payment for principal and interest.

Any real estate agent can give you a pretty good idea of how much your property taxes will be. And an insurance agent can very quickly give you a ballpark figure for your fire and liability insurance. (Yes, with rentals you definitely also will need liability insurance.)

The remainder of your expenses are variable. By the way, "variable" does not mean that you may or may not incur them. It means that while they will definitely be there, the amounts will vary month-to-month and year-to-year.

Maintenance
The biggest unknown factor is maintenance. You won't know what's going to break until it does. However, you can pretty much guess that the older the property, the more maintenance it will require. Here's a rule of thumb for maintenance costs on rental property:

Maintenance Costs Versus Age of Property

Age of Property	Maintenance as a Percentage of Monthly Income
0–10	5%
10–25	10%
25–older	15–20%

As you can see, the allowance for maintenance goes up with the age of the property.

TIP

Always try to buy newer properties. You'll save a fortune on maintenance costs.

Vacancies

Then there are vacancies. No property is rented all of the time. If you're a good landlord and on top of things, however, it can be rented almost all of the time. A good rule of thumb for a good landlord to use is that the property will be vacant at least two to four weeks out of each year (assuming you've picked a strong rental market and that you actively participate in getting tenants).

Other Costs

Of course, there are yet other costs. You will want to figure what your time managing the property is worth (or the cost of hiring professional management) and then there may be costs of fix-up if the property is run down when you purchase it. These are discussed in Part 3.

Most novice investors figure PITI, but then overlook all of the other costs simply because it's so hard to find a rental property that makes enough income to cover them. Nevertheless, it's better to spend more time looking, than to keep taking money out of your pocket every month.

Rule #7—Go for Favorable Terms

Sellers are often hung up on price. They may be convinced that lowering price is the absolute last resort.

If that's the case, don't try moving a stone wall. Go around it. Offer the seller the price he or she wants, but insist on favorable terms.

For example, at the price asked, it may be impossible to buy the property, rent it out, and break even monthly. (The ratio noted above in Rule #4 simply doesn't work here.) However, the sellers may have a large equity in the property. So, instead of getting a new mortgage from an institution, you demand the sellers themselves carry back a mortgage at 6 percent instead of the then going rate of 9 percent. Suddenly your mortgage payments are cut by a third! Now the price/rent ratio falls into line.

If the sellers protest, you can point out that you're paying full price. Many sellers, being penny-wise and pound foolish, will go along.

Terms are critical. Often you can give the seller his or her price and still get a bargain by negotiating for more favorable terms for yourself.

Rule #8—Never Pay an Inflated Price

In Rule #7 we saw how terms could be manipulated to make a high price palatable. The point now is to make sure that no matter what price you get, it's at or below market. If you pay too much, you'll lose when it comes time to sell. Remember, you make your profit when you buy, not when you sell.

True value is hardest to judge in a rising real estate market. However, checking comparable sales remains your biggest help. Typically houses are selling rapidly, and there are many sales of homes similar to the one which you are considering buying. You can look at comparables and see what price houses recently have been selling for, to get an idea of what your subject house is worth.

TIP

Get an agent to do a CMA (Comparative Market Analysis). It will show all comps, their list and sales prices, features, and so on. It's very helpful when trying to determine value. Also, check www.monsterdata.com. For between $5 and $10 you can get a list of comps for most homes.

The real trick is trying to decide how much the rising market adds to the value of the home in question. My suggestion is to play the percentages. If property values are rising 6 percent a year and it's been four months since the last comparable was sold, add about 2 percent (one third of a year's increase) for appreciation. That's just a rule of thumb, but it ought to get you pretty close to the current market value of the property.

You can determine how hot the market is by checking with local brokers and even the local newspapers. They are always giving out the statistics for overall price appreciation in the area, particularly when it's on the way up.

Rule #9—Always Lowball the Seller

My suggestion is that you always lowball sellers. This means offering way below what they are asking. How far below? An offer that is 10 percent below asking price is not unreasonable from an investor. Offers of as much as 25 to 30 percent below asking price are not uncommon.

TIP

If you think that lowballing only works in a cold market, you'd be making a mistake. It's definitely harder in a hot market, and you'll certainly have to raise the amount you offer, nevertheless, if you play the percentages, you'll eventually find a seller willing to take less, sometimes significantly less, than asking price. See the next chapter for tips on how to do this.

Lowballing is a technique that some investors have worked out to perfection. It requires two elements: persistence and guts.

The persistence is required because you won't get a seller to accept every time, or every other time, or even every fifth or perhaps tenth time. You have to be willing to make offers that get turned down time and again. You have to be willing to keep on trying until you finally hit the right seller.

TRAP

Don't fall in love with an investment house. When you buy to live in, you're allowed to fall in love with the house. When you buy to invest, you're not. An investment house is strictly a business proposition. One house is as good as another and you simply want one that will meet your financial and economic criteria. Never mind the cute archway in the living room or the adorable French windows. The questions you need to ask have to do with price, terms, rentability, and ultimate resale. Leave your heart at home when buying investment property. Bring only your head.

Guts come in because you have to be willing to accept a lot of criticism. Real estate brokers will criticize your actions. (This is only natural since, in most cases, they represent sellers, and they don't get paid a commission unless there's a sale. They don't like making lots of unsuccessful offers.)

You also have to have the courage to try and try again even after many offers are rejected. Remember, every dollar below market you buy a property for, is a dollar of profit in your pocket.

Never be sympathetic to the seller who wants more money. Helping a seller to make more money on the sale may be a generous, altruistic act. But, it really doesn't make good business sense.

Rule #10—Never Buy Far from Home

I like to think that after a great many years in real estate, I've made all of the mistakes. This is one of the biggest—fortunately, I made it early on and didn't repeat it.

Never buy far from home if you're going to rent out the property. If you do, I can almost guarantee you'll regret it. (By the way, this doesn't apply if you're going to flip a property—then you can buy anywhere.)

When you invest in real estate as a small investor, you are directly involved in management. You are the person who has to solve the day-to-day problems.

If you're far away, even small tasks can mushroom into big problems. A leaky faucet means an expensive call to a plumber. A broken window, electrical plug that doesn't work, fallen shutter, lawn that needs mowing—you name it—all require calls to professionals.

If there are big problems, such as tenants who won't pay, then you must fly or drive miles to solve them (or hire an expensive property management company to do it for you).

On the other hand, if you're close by, you can put an ad in the paper and do it all yourself. If a tenant doesn't pay, you can be right there to talk with the tenant to find out what the problem is, and correct it. If plumbing, gardening, electrical, or other small work needs to be done, you can do it yourself, or find a close-by person to help with it.

In short, it's vitally important to be right on the spot when you have a real estate problem.

I have a real estate attorney friend who handles hundreds of units. He gave me the only exception to the above rule. It's this—if you have 20 units or more, then you can handle it as an absentee land-lord. With that many units as a minimum, you can afford to hire a good manager who will take good care of your property. With less than 20 units, however, you can't afford a manager. Consequently, you need to do it yourself.

It's important not to get the wrong message, here. I'm not saying that renting real estate is an impossible task. It's not: 95 percent of all problems can be handled in just a few minutes. If you're there, you can pick the right tenants. You can do minor work yourself. You can hire out major work to people who you know or to people you can get recommendations on.

In short, being there makes the difference. After my own first mistake in buying property a state away, I have rented many other properties for dozens of years and have never come across a problem I couldn't quickly and easily handle myself.

These then are the 10 rules to observe when buying investment property. If you take them to heart, profits should not be far away.

4

Making Lowball Offers That Get Accepted

As an investor, never pay the asking price (unless a foolish seller is asking below market—a real rarity!). Sellers almost universally ask more than they are willing to take for their homes. They expect to come down some, hence the above market asking price. If you pay what the seller is asking, you're wasting your money. Remember, the less you pay for the property, the greater your profit when you sell.

TIP

In hot markets, houses sometimes go for full price or even more. If you're investing, that's usually a market to stay away from, unless you think the price is going to rapidly go up even further.

The real trick is knowing how much less than asking price a seller will take. Sometimes a seller will only come down a few thousand dollars. Other times they may drop 10 percent or more. And, of course, there's that occasional seller who refuses to come down a dime. How do you know one from the other?

Unless you have supernatural powers (or the seller's agent spills the beans), you *don't* know. That means you have to learn through the negotiating process. Your offer and each counter-offer the sellers make tells you more. Eventually, if you're a good negotiator, you will have gotten the lowest possible price.

How Do I Begin
Negotiations?

It all starts out with a low-bid. (You can't very well go lower after you've previously made a high bid; you would lose credibility and lose the seller's interest.)

My own rule of thumb is to always offer at least 5 percent less than the asking price for investment homes. Notice that I said "at least." That means that you won't offer a price that is higher than 5 percent below market, but you might well want to offer a price that is far lower than 5 percent below market.

How much less depends on several factors including:

The Market—Is it hot or cold? You can always expect to pay less in a cold market.

The Property—Is it just a run-of-the-mill investment, or does it have phenomenal potential? If it's common, offer less, far less. If it's exceptional, you'll want to offer more. Keep in mind that the more run-down the property is, the less it's likely to bring. The more spruced up it is, the higher the price.

The Asking Price—Is it right at the market value, or is it higher or lower? If the house is already priced below market, you may want to offer closer to full price. If it's priced above market (which most houses usually are), you'll want to offer much less.

Your Perspective—Remember, you can make money in real estate simply by paying full price and holding onto the property. If you're satisfied doing this, offer just 5 percent below market. However, if you've decided to be a cutthroat investor, offer far less.

How Do You Know
What the Home's True
Market Value Is?

Learning this is a good starting point. Begin by going to an agent or checking at one of the many Internet websites that offer comparative market analysis (CMA) figures (check out www.monsterdata.com.) The analysis takes a look at all similar homes sold within the previous six months (or perhaps a year) within the area. You then compare the sold homes and prices with the subject home and its asking price. Add for extra features the subject home has. Subtract for features the sold properties have that the subject home lacks. By comparison, you can quickly determine the market value of the property.

Keep in mind, however, that a CMA only tells you what homes sold for a few months to about a year ago. It usually doesn't tell you what they're selling for right now. In a rising market, you have to add a certain percentage for recent appreciation. As described in the last chapter, find out what the increase is and then add that to the CMA price. (Usually the increase is given as an annual figure. Divide that by 12 months and then add the amount for however many months it's been since the latest comparable sale.)

How Much to Lowball?

Now, decide on how much to lowball. You may want to offer as much as 25 percent or more below the asking price. However, that's usually just a test-offer, trying to see what the water's like. In all but a very cold market, a seller's likely to simply reject it out of hand. Indeed, the seller may simply ignore the offer and not counter it. That defeats your purpose. The goal of the initial lowball is to get a counter-offer from the seller. Try to offer enough to entice the seller to at least respond.

The counter-offer can be very revealing. If it's just a thousand dollars or so off the asking price (or right at the asking price), you can assume that this seller won't budge much. Then it's time to fish or cut bait. Either move up to the seller's price, or move on.

TIP

The way to succeed is to make lots (dozens) of lowball offers, playing the odds until you chance upon a seller who, for one reason or another, is willing to drop the price.

On the other hand, when the seller's counter drops the price significantly, you know you've got a fish hooked on the line. Now it's a matter of negotiating the lowest possible price.

What Do You Counter-Offer?

After a seller counters at a significantly lower price (but not as low as you've originally offered), you've really got only three alternatives:

1. Accept the seller's counter, if you think it's low enough.
2. Counter at a still lower price, typically half-way between your original offer and the seller's first counter-offer. (You can't both accept and counter; countering can cost you the deal.)
3. Repeat your original offer, if you think it's a good price.

Compromising at half-way between the seller's last offer and your original offer (#2 above) may land the deal. Or the seller may cut the remaining distance in half again with yet another counter. Either way, you're well along toward getting the home at a reasonable price.

Sticking to your original offer (reoffering it as your first counter) has some negotiating drawbacks. It tells the seller to take it or leave it. It says you're not willing to compromise.

A certain percentage of the time (no one knows how much, but it's not high), you'll win by holding pat. The seller will indeed capitulate and accept your original offer. This usually only happens, however, in a cold market and with a desperate seller.

More likely the seller will simply throw up his or her hands and say there's no dealing with you, and then simply walk away. After all, if you don't raise your offer, what choice have you left the seller but to take your offer or quit?

My suggestion is that unless you think your original lowball offer is actually realistic, always counter the seller's counter, even if you only come up a thousand dollars or so. It keeps the negotiations open. And gives the seller another chance to come down even more!

Eventually, you'll get the house you want at the price you want to pay. Or you'll move on.

Never Get Attached to a Property

There's a very old rule in life that goes something like this, "Business is business and personal is personal and the two should never mix."

That's not such good advice when seeking financing, as we'll see later. However, it's excellent advice when making offers on property. When buying an investment, the last thing you want is an emotional attachment.

TRAP

Always remember that you're not going to live in the property, a tenant is. Furthermore, you're eventually going to sell. Therefore, buy with an eye to what a tenant will accept (making it easiest for you to maintain) and what a new owner will like.

While this might sound obvious, it's difficult to execute. For example, you're looking at a lovely little cottage with an adorable white picket fence in front, French windows all around, lush white carpeting inside, and tile countertops in the kitchen and bath. To you it looks like a wonderful place to live. So, when the owner wants a few thousand more than the market will bear for the place, you're willing to pop for it. After all, it's something you simply must have.

Mistake. Bad, mistake.

While if you lived there, you might keep repainting that fence white, never break one of the French window panels, take your shoes off before walking on the carpeting, and scrub the grout between tiles, don't expect a tenant to do the same thing. Remember, unless it's a flipper, you're planning to rent it out for awhile, at least until prices go up and you sell. That means you're looking for LOW maintenance. All of the items just mentioned are high maintenance.

What you want is a property that doesn't require constant repainting, that when a window breaks, it's easy and relatively inexpensive to replace, with carpeting (probably beige or brown) that doesn't show dirt, and with formica or other solid surface countertops that won't get stained (and require expensive regrouting).

All of which is to say, look at each property with an investor's eye, not a home-buyer's eye. It's not for you to live in; therefore, it does not have to meet your personal standards. All it has to do is make good business sense.

TIP

When you tour properties, bring an electronic calculator along. Every time you see a feature you like, add (or subtract) the realistic difference it will make for renting and later, for reselling. Doing this will help keep you honest and less emotionally involved.

How Big a Down Payment Should I Make?

For most people, this is not a difficult decision. Most real estate investors have very little cash, consequently they are always looking for low down payment properties, the lower the better. (We'll see about low down payments in the next section.) However, some of those new to investing worry that a low down payment accompanying a lowball offer will scare a seller into declining. Put up a big down payment, they reason, and the seller will be more inclined to accept a lower offer.

Not true; not even close to true.

Unless there's creative financing involved, where the seller is putting up the money for you to purchase the home (check into Chapter 14), the deal is always all cash to the seller. It doesn't matter whether you put 30 percent down or 5 percent down! (The only party it makes a difference to is the lender, who will determine the minimum down payment for you.)

As a consequence, as long as you can come up with a letter from a lender showing that you are approved for the required financing, the seller won't care a whit how big a down payment you're offering.

Therefore, it's to your advantage to put as little down as possible.

TIP

The financing rule in real estate is whenever possible, use OPM (Other People's Money)!

Many new investors will argue against putting a minimal down payment into an investment property, worrying about the higher monthly payments this will cause. They realize that the less of your cash you put into the property, the higher your monthly payments will be. Contrarily, the more cash you put in, the lower will be your monthly payments. One way to avoid creating an alligator, they reason, is to put enough money into the property to get the monthly payments (expenses) down to the point where rental income will cover them. That way you can keep the property over a long period of time and not have to worry about negative cash flow.

Again, that's a mistake.

TIP

The rule is don't put more money into an investment house to get a lower payment. Instead, find a different, less expensive, better-financed investment house.

If it's your own home, it may indeed make good sense to put more cash down. Most people like the security a low monthly house payment affords. But, it doesn't make sense for an investment property. Rather, look for a home with higher rental income.

Remember, if you put 5 percent down and the property goes up 5 percent, you've made a 100 percent profit. But, if you put 20 percent down and the property goes up 5 percent, you've only made a 25 percent profit.

At 20 percent down it will take you four times longer to make the same profit as with 5 percent down.

Further, keep in mind that the more money you stick into a property, the less you have available to invest elsewhere. If you have $40,000 and put 20 percent down on a $200,000 home, you've used up all of your cash (ignoring transaction costs, for the moment).

On the other hand, if you only put 10 percent down ($20,000), you still have half your cash left to buy yet another home! (If you can get away with only 5 percent cash down, you could theoretically buy four homes!) The more homes, the more profit.

What About Reserves?

Providing you find the right property, putting the smallest amount down works best with investment property. That doesn't mean, however, that you invest all of your cash in real estate. Common sense dictates that you always keep a reserve in case of emergencies. I, personally, tend to be conservative and keep a reserve of about 25 percent cash. That way I'm solvent and can handle almost anything the market throws at me.

Other investors who are more daring only keep about 10 or even 5 percent of their working capital in reserve. They are less prepared for a long vacancy period, a big repair bill, or even a downturn in the market. On the other hand, they make bigger profits as long as things go well.

TIP

I believe that the amount of cash reserve that you keep must be determined by your sleep index. If it keeps you up at night worrying, your reserves are too low. Increase them until you can sleep comfortably. That's the right amount.

By the way, your reserves don't need to be in the form of actual cash. They can be in any form that can be quickly converted to cash. That includes:

Savings

Bonds

Stocks

Lines of Credit (A line of credit is one where you can draw cash out as needed and pay back as desired. These are easy to place on properties on which you have large equities. If it's a home you occupy, they are called home equity loans.)

5

Profit Strategy 1—Bargains from Motivated Sellers

Half the battle in finding property bargains is judging the seller. In today's market you not only have to know what the realistic price for a property is, you have to find a seller who is motivated enough to accept that price.

TIP

Typically most sellers have dollar signs dancing in their heads after having read how far prices have advanced in recent years. Unfortunately, many take projections of future value and bring them into the present. They truly believe that their house is worth today what it might be worth in a few years. Don't cater to their false beliefs.

Thus, in order for you to get a bargain price you need to find a seller who is forced to look at prices as they are, not as they will be, or as he or she hopes they may be. There are at least six good seller motivations to look for:

Seller Motivations to Look For

1. The seller is making a job change to a different area, necessitating a rapid move.

2. The seller has bought another home and has to quickly sell this one in order to close the deal on the next.

3. The seller has lost his or her job or for other reasons is in financial difficulty and needs to get out quick.

4. The seller wants to "move up" to a bigger house or to a better area. (This is usually a low motivation.)

5. The seller has some other problem such as a divorce and simply must get rid of the house immediately.

6. For one reason or another the seller can't make the payments on the property and must sell soon or lose it.

TIP

The best motivations involve speed. The quicker a seller must act, the more motivated he or she will be.

In each of the above cases the seller must get out. As a result, he or she will be more willing to accept a realistic price (or offer better terms) because of that motivation. However, unless the seller has one of the above motivations (or one of similar intensity), your chances of getting the house at a bargain price may be just about nil. Without motivation the seller will simply sit and wait for a better buyer (read one who offers more money) to come by.

How Do You Find Out the Seller's Motivation?

How do you find out what the seller's motivation really is? Most sellers believe as a cardinal rule in selling real estate that you should always keep up the best front. That's the way to get your price. If you let a potential buyer know you're motivated, you'll get a lower offer. So, how do you, as a buyer, find out which sellers are highly motivated?

The answer is simple. Motivated sellers always tell you they are motivated!

Why would a seller break the cardinal rule? The reason is that highly motivated sellers want out, now. They realize that it's no longer a matter of waiting to get the best price; they just want to sell.

Most very quickly realize that keeping their need to get out to themselves won't do the trick anymore. The only way they can get out is if they let every potential buyer, everyone who is even remotely a potential buyer, know their situation.

As a result, it's not a secret. If the house is listed, ask the real estate broker. A highly motivated seller will instruct the broker to "Find any buyer. Tell them that I'm highly motivated! Get me any offer!"

Check with Brokers

The real estate broker will move on these words. Any agent worth his or her salt knows that a motivated seller means a quick sale. The broker will alert every potential buyer, including you, that this seller wants out.

Consequently, your first source of motivated sellers is the real estate broker.

TRAP

As opposed to a personal residence buyer who should work with only one agent at a time, as an investment buyer it's usually a good idea to let as many agents as possible know that you're looking. That way you increase the odds one or another will find the type of motivated seller you want. However, keep in mind that agents value honesty and loyalty in clients. Therefore, be up front about it. Let them know you're working with others. That way they won't spend as much time on you, but will keep you in mind if what you're looking for shows up. On the other hand, if you find one agent who is particularly well connected, you may want to work exclusively with that agent.

Won't Agents Buy All the Good Properties?

There's nothing you can do about this, so don't worry about it. My experience, however, has been that most agents would rather get a commission than buy an investment house. They'll buy investment property only when they can't find a buyer for it.

The exception to this is flippable property. If the agent feels he or she can buy the property and quickly resell for a big profit, they may do it. However, agents have special problems in flipping. If they buy themselves and then quickly resell for a profit, the seller may feel cheated. The seller may feel that the agent wasn't fulfilling his or her fiduciary relationship. And that seller can do nasty things such as calling the state regulatory board or even taking legal action.

If the agent is foolhardy enough to "double escrow" the property (in essence, concealing the resale from the original seller), the sale might even be illegal. And few agents would dare to risk the consequences of such action.

Therefore, while it is true that in a hot market agents will sometimes pick the cream of the crop, there's usually still plenty of good properties out there to go around.

Check with Sellers

Remember, a good way to find out a seller's motivation is to point blank ask. You can do this in a friendly fashion while you tour the house. It's really quite simple. Very frequently when you look at a house, the seller will be there. Just begin a conversation and ask why that seller wants to sell.

If the sellers hedge or hem and haw or give a reason that is not indicative of strong motivation, pass. On the other hand, as noted earlier, motivated sellers are very likely to simply let you know that they are extremely eager to get a deal. They may say something like "Make me an offer" or "Let's talk. If you're interested, put it in writing. I'm very anxious to get out of here." The motivated seller will seldom try to hide his or her eagerness. Rather, they will do everything to let you know just how they feel.

Check with Neighbors

Ask around. Oftentimes neighbors are an excellent source of information. And neighbors may feel little loyalty to the existing owner who is selling and leaving the neighborhood.

Of course, this is not an invitation to be a snoop or to invade anyone's privacy. However, I always suggest that anyone who is interested in buying a property always talk to the neighbors first. (It's a lot easier on the nervous system to learn there is a bad neighbor next door before you buy, rather than after.) As part of your conversation with the neighbor, you will certainly ask about the house, the neighborhood, and eventually the conversation will drift over to the seller. The neighbor may volunteer some critical information as to why the seller is getting out.

Motivated Sellers in Foreclosure

Thus far, we've been assuming that we will find motivated sellers who have their homes listed for sale. But what about sellers who haven't been able to sell their homes for one reason or another and are now in foreclosure? They are the most motivated of all to sell, and they, on occasion, may be able to present some terrific bargain opportunities to you. We'll discuss these in more detail in the next chapter.

Getting the Bargain

How do you get a bargain out of a motivated seller? It's simple. You begin by lowballing (Chapter 3), and then you stick to your guns. The key here is that you now know that your seller is desperate to move the property. Suddenly your own strategy clicks into place. You can afford to be hard-nosed. At every turn, you refuse to knuckle under to the seller's demands. Instead, you make the demands. From an ego standpoint, it's a wonderful position to be in.

A word of caution, however. In a strong market even a highly motivated seller isn't going to be willing to cave into your every demand. The seller will know that if you don't buy this property, another buyer will likely come along shortly. Thus, you would be wise to make your demands reasonable.

6

Profit Strategy 2— Finding and Buying Foreclosures

Everyone who's ever dabbled in real estate has heard about foreclosures. This is where the lender takes the property back from an owner/borrower who can't make the payments. There are supposed to be wonderful bargains in foreclosures.

In fact there are, if you know where to look and how to deal with them. That's what we'll discover in this chapter. To begin, however, it's important to understand how foreclosure works. It's somewhat different state by state, but the process overall is much the same in most areas of the country. There are essentially three stages.

How Foreclosure Works

Stage 1 The seller can't or won't make payments for whatever reason and the lender puts the mortgage in default.

Stage 2 After a legally determined period of time the lender "sells" the property to the highest bidder "on the court house steps."

Stage 3 Typically the lender is the highest bidder. The lender takes control of the property and now attempts to resell it as an REO (Real Estate Owned). This will be discussed in Chapter 8.

What we're concerned with here is **Stage 1**. The seller can't or won't make payments. He or she is motivated to sell the property, hoping to recoup any equity and save a credit rating. This seller is, at least, going to listen to any offer that you make.

Why Are Sellers in Foreclosure?

In a strong market, one would think that there simply aren't any sellers in foreclosure. That's simply not the case. The foreclosure rate in good times may be half of what it is in bad times. But at any time there are still plenty of foreclosures. Sellers are always losing property. Some of the more common reasons include:

- The seller has overborrowed and can't make the payments.

- There is an illness, death, or divorce in the family and no one takes charge of maintaining the property, allowing it to fall through the cracks into foreclosure.

- The seller moved and listed the house. But the agent was terrible and no buyers were found, and now the seller, at a distance, just won't or can't deal with the house anymore.

- The seller simply doesn't care about the property (rare, but it does happen).

Where Can I Find Foreclosures?

One place to find properties in foreclosure is to look for "For Sale By Owner" signs (FSBOs). Sometimes this person has decided to forego the traditional listing process and dispose of the property on his or her own. (It may have been listed, but the listing expired with no results.) Now facing foreclosure, the owner is at a final desperate stage.

Typically such FSBO efforts are nonproductive and may be done halfheartedly as the house moves closer to foreclosure. In fact the only efforts may be a sign in the front yard that says, "For Sale By Owner."

Once you've determined *where* you want to buy your investment house, begin touring the area. Drive up and down the streets. Chances are you'll run into an occasional FSBO. Stop, introduce yourself and talk to the seller. You will most often find that the seller is trying to sell FSBO just to prevent having to pay a commission. When he or she can't sell FSBO (more than half the time), the seller will list with an agent. There's no foreclosure here.

However, occasionally you will find someone selling FSBO who actually is in foreclosure. When you do, you've got your motivated seller.

What About Agent Foreclosures?

Another source for foreclosure information are agents. Agents will know if any of their sellers are in foreclosure.

Of course, there is the chance that the agents will attempt to buy the property themselves or "give" it to a relative or friend. That, of course, is why you need to know many agents. You can be that lucky person.

Are There Title Company Foreclosures?

Title insurance and trust companies also know about foreclosures. This is particularly the case in states which use the "trust deed" device instead of the older "mortgage" device. (Currently over 40 states use the trust deed as the preferred lending device.)

To understand why, it's important to know that in a traditional mortgage there are two parties—the borrower and the lender. To foreclose, the lender must begin legal proceedings in court.

With a trust deed, however, there are three parties. The borrower (trustor), the lender (beneficiary), and the trustee. When the lender loans money to the borrower, the borrower gives to that third party, the trustee, the right to sell that house if he or she doesn't keep up the payments on that loan. The trustee, in short, holds the foreclosure power.

When the borrower doesn't pay, the lender notifies the trustee that the borrower is in default, and the trustee begins foreclosure proceedings.

Now, here's the important part with regard to finding properties in trust deed foreclosure. The trustee named in the trust deed is usually a title insurance and trust company. These companies are set up to handle the position of trustee and to handle foreclosures, which is why they are so named by most lenders.

Hence, if you become known to a title insurance and trust company, they may be willing to let you have a list of properties they have put into foreclosure. They do not widely advertise or disseminate such lists, but instead make them available to their clients and "friends." (A goodly number of investors have gotten rich in the past simply by becoming fast friends with a title insurance company officer.)

Of course, there's nothing secret about such a list. It's just most convenient to get it from a title insurance company. If you can't, however, there is another alternative.

What About Foreclosures in the Newspaper?

There are newspapers that post legal notices. The first step in foreclosure usually is the filing of a notice of default. This notice must be filed with the county recorder's office. (This applies to mortgages as well as trust deeds.) You could always spend some time at the county recorder's office checking for notices of default that have been filed. Few of us, however, have such time to spend.

Another alternative may be to check the "legal newspaper" in your area. Most larger areas will have a newspaper whose sole purpose is to carry legal notices. If you've only subscribed to the larger consumer newspapers, you may have never heard of it. But a call to any title insurance company officer or the county clerk's office will confirm its existence and probably get you a number to call.

The legal newspapers are filled with legal notices such as "dba" (doing business as) notifications or other items that people are legally required to publish. In addition they publish such items as notices of default.

Of course, one of the problems with checking these notices (as well as the notices filed with the county clerk) is that they tend to give the "legal description" of the property. Instead of 256 Orange Street, they may give a tract, block, and map number. Unless you're able to read recorded maps, such information isn't all that helpful.

Are There Private List Foreclosures?

Which brings us to yet another source. Usually advertised in legal newspapers are private listing companies which, for a fee, will sell you a list of properties in foreclosure, giving their common street address and sometimes the name and phone number of the owner. Be aware, however, that this list is frequently costly, often more than a hundred dollars per month. (Which is why it's nice to have a friend at a title insurance company who can get you such a list for free!). Just call up and subscribe as you would to any other service.

Are There Lender Foreclosures?

Lenders are not usually a good source of foreclosure information.

Usually in any given area there are one or two large savings and loans or banks that handle a large percentage of the area mortgages. These lenders, consequently, also end up taking back many of the properties that go into foreclosure.

Each lender has a foreclosure department. Most lenders, however, are reluctant to release lists of properties on which they are foreclosing, for reasons discussed shortly. But, having a friend in such a department who is willing to share the foreclosure pending list with you can prove to be a very profitable relationship.

How Do I Deal with an Owner in Foreclosure?

Once you find someone who is in foreclosure, it's now up to you to contact them directly and find out if there is a good deal available for you. Hopefully you already have a name and phone number. Now, just give this person a call. Explain that you're an investor and that you're looking for property in the area. You heard they were having some difficulty in making payments and you're wondering if there's a way to make a "win-win" situation out of it. They save their credit (plus, perhaps, some money, depending on their equity), and you get the property.

TIP

At the least, you'll have an address. A reverse phone book may give you a name and number, or you can always stop by and knock on the door.

Be forewarned. Some people won't want to talk with you. They may be nasty, even offensive. They usually take their foreclosure personally and may blame everyone but themselves for it. Forget them. They can't be helped and most likely will lose their house and their credit.

Others will be happy, even eager to talk. Those are the ones you want to work with. When you find such an owner you have to determine what it's going to cost you to take over the property.

What Are the Costs of Righting a Foreclosure?

What you can offer to the owner is to make up the back payments and penalties and save the owner's credit rating in exchange for the title to the property. In other words, you can offer to take it over. The advantage here is that you get the property for virtually no money down plus whatever equity the owner may have. The disadvantage is that the loan may not be assumable. If that's the case, you may not only have to make up back payments and penalties, but also secure a new loan with accompanying points and fees.

In short, it may cost you many thousands of dollars to take over this property and bail out this owner. You may find that by the time you add up the costs, it simply isn't worthwhile.

Potential Costs Involved in Righting a Foreclosure

1. Back payments (could be six months of payments, or more).
2. Penalties (Each month that the payment is late usually incurs a penalty. In addition there may be additional penalties as time periods in the foreclosure process expire.)

3. New loan costs including points, fees, title insurance, etc. (Typically this will be about 5 percent of the loan amount on a $100,000 mortgage figure, about $5,000.)

4. Fixing up the property. The former owner may not have kept the place in great shape once he or she learned they were going to lose it. You may have to spend several thousand on refurbishing and relandscaping.

It's important that you calculate these costs as accurately as possible before you make any kind of offer to the owner. You may find that it simply isn't worth your time to attempt to right the foreclosure and take over the property. Here's an example.

Julia's House

Peter bought his southern California home in 1993, right at the height of the last boom in prices. He put 10 percent down and took out a big mortgage for the balance.

Everything seemed rosy until Peter and his wife divorced. It was a rather nasty divorce that took a long time. Along the way, Peter lost his job, and his wife, who did not work, could not make the payments on the property. It was the year 2000 and the property had finally bounced back to its initial value after the great housing recession of the mid-1990s. It was now worth $400,000.

Peter had listed the property, but had put an unrealistic price of $450,000 on it. As a consequence, he had received no offers.

The listing had also expired and Peter, angry at the broker for not bringing in any buyers, decided to try to sell for himself and, at the least, save the commission. Time, however, was passing and without payments being made, the lender put the home into foreclosure. Peter had about two weeks left before he would lose the property. Julia came along about this time.

Julia was an investor with good credit who had lined up lenders and who was looking for foreclosures. Peter's name had popped up on a list of properties in foreclosure and she gave him a call. He seemed pleased to talk about his problems, so she went to see him.

The property was in a good tenant market and Peter was certainly a motivated seller. So Julia was excited about the prospects and began to figure out the costs involved:

Costs Involved in Correcting the Foreclosure

1. 3 months back payments	$7,500
2. Penalties	400
3. Fixing up the house	1,100
4. Securing new loan	12,000 (Peter's old loan was not assumable)
Total Cost	21,000

It would cost Julia roughly $21,000 to pay off Peter's existing loan (including back payments and penalties) and other costs. The current mortgage was $350,000 and the house was worth $400,000, so the bottom line was that if she did this, she'd have an instant equity of roughly $30,000 in the home. For her it was a no-brainer. So she paid to have a title search to see who really owned the property. It turned out it was still in both Peter and his wife's name, so she would need two signatures on a purchase.

TIP

One of the big problems dealing with foreclosures is guaranteeing the title. In a standard sale, almost always a title insurance company looks at the title and guarantees it to the new buyer. In a foreclosure, it is up to the investor to see to it that the title is clear. Buying title insurance as additional protection is always a good idea.

However, there was the matter of convincing Peter. From Peter's perspective, he had roughly $50,000 in equity. He wanted someone to pay him this full amount to take over his house.

Julia thought about it, then made Peter this offer.

Julia's Offer

If Peter would sign the house over to Julia, she would pay off the old loan and all the back payments, penalties, and interest. (She would do this by securing a new loan with her good credit, but that was none of Peter's business.) Peter would walk away free and clear, his credit intact.

Peter blew up at this. He accused Julia of trying to steal his home. Where, he wanted to know, was his equity?

Julia responded that Peter's equity was not the issue, it was his good name. His equity was lost because with his bad credit, caused by his divorce and job loss, he could not refinance. Also, he could not sell. He had tried that route without success. Further, within two weeks the foreclosure process would be completed and Peter would not only lose his home, but his good name as well. That could adversely affect his ability to obtain credit for decades to come. Julia could make all of this go away.

Peter said he'd think about it. He did. He called Julia a week later, with foreclosure staring him in the face only days away and said he'd make the deal, IF she'd give him $5,000 for his equity.

Julia, agreed, providing she could get financing in time to stave off the foreclosure. Julia had it all put in writing in the form of a purchase agreement drawn up by an attorney and had Peter and his wife both sign (which took an extra day).

TIP

When dealing with people in foreclosure, leave nothing to the spoken word. It should be in writing, properly written and signed. Further, when dealing with anyone involved in a divorce, make sure that both parties sign.

Julia then immediately went to the existing lender who agreed to extend the foreclosure procedure for two weeks for a partial payment of the amount owed. She then proceeded to secure electronic quick funding of a new mortgage, took title to the property, and paid off the old loan and foreclosure costs. Her only problem was getting Peter to leave. She had to give him an extra $500 to move out!

Nevertheless, she had quickly purchased an investment house with $25,000 in equity.

TIP

While the above example illustrates an essentially "win-win" situation, it isn't always that way. Some states have enacted laws protecting those in foreclosure from being preyed upon by fortune hunters. Typically the problem is that the buyer purchases the home for significantly less than the seller paid for it. (Julia bought the house for roughly the same price that Peter paid.) Such laws allow a certain period of time for rescission of a sales agreement when the seller is in default on a mortgage. The period of time can vary from a few days to as long as six months or more after the sale! If you buy a house in foreclosure unaware of these protective laws, you could later find the original seller coming back and demanding you return the home! That's one reason that before you attempt to buy a home from a seller who is in foreclosure, check with a good real estate attorney in your state who might be able to protect you against such problems.

Advantages of Dealing with Owners in Foreclosure

The obvious advantage of dealing with an owner in foreclosure is that you can get a property at the right price for the current market. If the house happens to be run down and in need of repair, you may get a price far below market. In short, dealing with owners in foreclosure is a way of finding bargain properties.

Buying at a Foreclosure Sale

Another way of purchasing a property is by actually buying it when it is sold "on the courthouse steps." At the time of the foreclosure sale, the lender always offers the full price of the mortgage (or trust deed). But there is nothing to prevent you or anyone else from offering more.

Your offer, however, must be in the form of cash, so you will have to work out financing in advance. And you will receive no title insurance or other guarantees as to the status of the property. (You might, for example, think you're bidding on a first mortgage only to find that it's a second or third. This could be catastrophic for you.)

It is beyond the scope of this book to go into detail on buying homes at foreclosure auctions. Suffice to say that it is usually the venue of attorneys and those well versed in real estate practice and law. It can also be a highly profitable area. If you are interested in it, you might consider consulting with a real estate attorney in your area who specializes in the field.

As we've seen, buying property in foreclosure is not without its risks. But, then again, it has its rewards. In Chapter 8 we'll go into finding properties in the final stage of foreclosure, when they are REOs offered by lenders.

7

Profit Strategy 3—Buying in Turnaround Areas

Not all properties appreciate in price at the same rate. Some go up much faster than others. Buy one of the fast properties and you'll profit more and quicker. That's what we're about in this chapter.

Los Angeles—A Case in Point

There were some people who made a killing in the real estate market between 1998 and 2000 in Los Angeles, California. It was not so much that they happened to be in the right place at the right time, but that they took advantage of a situation as it developed.

Back in 1998 the country, particularly Southern California, was just coming out of the worst real estate recession since the Great Depression. Property prices had declined roughly 25 percent during the previous seven years. There were those who said that the price of property would continue to go down, almost indefinitely. Of course, anyone with common sense knew that was simply nonsense.

Those who realized that prices had bottomed out began buying up property, mainly single-family homes, and mainly in higher-priced areas.

TIP

When prices turn up, it is often felt first in the premium properties, those at the top end of the spectrum. Then it works its way down to medium- and modest-priced properties.

In well-known areas such as Palos Verdes, Malibu, the West Side, and others, investors were buying up luxury homes in the $500,000 price range. Some were as low as $400,000. (That may not seem inexpensive compared to most areas of the country, but for the areas in question, it was bargain basement time.)

These investors then ruthlessly rented out these homes to make their payments. They simply sat on them and waited for times to change.

And change they did. Within two years, most of the luxury areas of Los Angeles made up all of the price declines and moved ahead of their previous all-time highs. Within a year or two, in fact, many of the original investors were looking at profits ranging from 40 to 60 percent! (Remember, when you factor in leverage—see Chapter 1—that's a true return of 400 to 600 percent!) This was at the same time that many more modestly priced properties had not yet risen in price to their previous highs from before the real estate recession.

Of course, if you weren't one of the winners described above, don't feel bad. Since then, most areas of the country have climbed aboard the bandwagon or gotten ahead of it. Some areas in California, Washington state, and Colorado have experienced price appreciations of 100 percent over three years (1,000 percent with leverage!), or more!

Further, the price increases are no longer limited to luxury properties. Increases are found up and down the spectrum from middle-class units to the least expensive properties.

Finding the Next Big Price-Jump Area

Of course, as noted, some areas move up faster than others. Parts of Denver, Colorado, and Sacramento, California, have seen price increases of 20 to 30 percent a year in residential real estate. [Parts of

California's Silicon Valley went up as much as 40 percent in a single year—400 percent after leverage! (before bottoming out)]

On the other hand, some areas in the South and Midwest have seen only a modest price increase, perhaps in the area of 5 to 7 percent.

Of course, if would be a mistake to think that hot areas are only regional by nature. Within any given city, there may be some neighborhoods which shoot up in price, while others simply mosey along. The real question becomes, how do you identify the next area to see more rapid price increases?

There are at least five different indicators, listed below, that suggest where and when an area is about to take off.

Price-Rise Indicators

1. Slower growth currently than other areas

2. High volume of resales

3. New development

4. In the direction of growth

5. Rapidly increasing prices

Comparatively Slow Growth

A slow growth area may be ripe for a turnaround. Or not. A lot depends on factors totally out of your control. For example, parts of some northeastern cities (such as Newark, New Jersey) which saw blighted areas for many years have been the target of renovation funds from government and private industry. This money, coupled with new jobs caused by a healthy economy, have caused some neighborhoods in these areas to turn around.

The key, for you, is to find such an area in the turnaround phase, and then buy it and hold. Within a few years, residential property values should increase.

Another key factor is close-in location. Between the 1950s and the 1990s, America expanded with new highways that led people to ever farther away neighborhoods. However, as the population has increased, the infrastructure of roads has become antiquated, unable to maintain the pace set by commuters. In Los Angeles, for example, the expected average speed on the freeways is anticipated to soon drop to under 10 miles per hour. People who used to commute between Stockton, California, and the Silicon Valley will find the ride could take up to four hours or more each way within a year or two (if not already).

In short, those old close-to-downtown neighborhoods that people abandoned only a few years ago are suddenly looking a whole lot better. People who are tired of fighting an impossible commute are coming back. All of which means that close-in properties are once again in fashion and are jumping up in value. Why not take advantage of it?

High Resale Volume

Regardless of what we just discussed, you don't want to be on the "bleeding edge" of the curve. You don't want to jump into a neighborhood that won't be renovated for 10 years. You want one that's already in the process of renovation.

How can you tell the difference? Look closely. In older areas of cities that are undergoing renovation, you'll see many buildings being refurbished. Indeed, in these areas a carpenter can be the hardest thing to find.

A more precise method of checking is to look at recent sales figures for residential property. What you want to see is a sudden hike in the number of sales. That indicates that the area has been "discovered" and investors and owners are pouring in.

TRAP

It's just as bad to be late as early. As people discover a new (old) area of town and pour in, the existing inventory of homes gets used up. This process can take anywhere from a few months to several years. While the unsold inventory exists, prices will remain stable. But, as soon as that old inventory is gone, price jumps will occur. You want to get in while that old inventory is still available.

New Developments

Brand new housing is often a great bargain. Buy it from the builder and just hold it. Within a few years it could be worth double what you paid!

Of course, not all new housing will rise so rapidly. Generally speaking you want new developments that are near major employers, to ensure a steady supply of employed buyers. Also, any new developments in already established areas (such as the last land available for residential construction in a small city) is usually a good buy.

One way to tell if your judgment is right is by the amount of competition for the housing. If there are buyers waiting in line to buy the new homes before they're even built, it's a good bet that it's a tract that will shoot up in value. On the other hand, if there are dozens of already built homes sitting idly waiting for buyers, reconsider. There may be some fatal flaw in the area that will keep it from going up in value. (In Phoenix, for example, for years new tracts languished because land was so cheap that even newer tracts nearby quickly made the older ones obsolete, keeping prices down.)

Buy in the Direction of Growth

John Astor's plan for making millions in New York City was simple: just buy property in the direction the city was growing (he bought dairy farms) and wait for the growth to reach you. When it does, sell for millions. (And he did.)

You can do the same thing. Only be *careful*. Growth has an annoying habit of changing directions. A city seems to be growing in one direction, only to reverse and go to the other side of town.

On thing you can watch for are large open spaces. New growth requires bigger stores, parking, and housing. That means LOTS of land. Generally speaking in today's world, you can go into almost any city and see which area offers the widest open space (even if there is no current development there) and within a few years, that's where everyone will want to be.

Be like Astor, and you can make millions, too.

Watch for Price Increases

Finally there's the lazy man's way to find neighborhoods that will boom. Simply watch for them!

No, it's not simple-minded. Local real estate boards, newspapers, and various Internet services (such as www.dataquick.com)

will frequently list price increases by city and sometimes, by neighborhood. Track them monthly.

If you're among the first to realize that one particular area is suddenly showing signs of rapid price increase, go there and check it out. You may find that it's a boom town in the making. ALL you'll need to do is buy a house or two to participate.

TIP

Remember, you don't have to be the first to buy a house in a booming area, just as you don't have to pick the bottom of the stock market to win. You just have to be one of the crowd who rides the wave to the top.

Be aware that some areas simply move up in price faster than others. That doesn't mean that if you buy wrong you'll lose. As we've seen, almost every area will eventually go up in value. You just want to be in those areas that do it the soonest.

8

Profit Strategy 4—
Working Lender-
Owned Properties

There's money to be made in lender-owned properties. These are usually houses or condos that have been foreclosed upon by a lender and are called REOs (Real Estate Owned).

Often these properties can be purchased for below market value, particularly if they are in distressed condition. Other times, although you might pay market value, the lender may offer special financing at a lower than market interest rate or with other appealing terms.

A friend of mine recently bought three REOs near Scottsdale, Arizona. All three had been owned by the same lender who made him a deal on the lot, two at market, one substantially below. My friend then flipped the below market property, fixed up the other two and rented them out. He intends to sell those within a year or two for a substantial profit. And he did it all with the lender's financing and almost no money of his own!

Can you do the same thing?

It could depend on how determined you are. REOs are a special part of the real estate market, one that, as we'll see, is covered in a blanket of secrecy.

Where Do REOs Come From?

There's an obvious difference between a lender and an investor, although most of us never give it a second thought. An investor, such as yourself, is a person who buys property and hopes to eventually

71

resell for a profit. A lender, such as a bank, loans out money hoping to receive interest in return. Most investors don't want to be lenders. And lenders, I can assure you, do not want to be investors.

Indeed, the only time banks and other lending institutions become investors is when their mortgages and other loans go bad. Then they are forced to foreclose and take the collateral, real estate in this case, back. These are called REO properties for "Real Estate Owned."

If you're a financial officer in a lending institution, REO are three letters you never want to hear. The reason is that while a performing mortgage (one where the borrower makes payments) is considered an asset, an REO is considered a liability. It moves from one side of the accounting books to the other and can adversely affect the lender's financial stability. Too many REOs and the lender goes bankrupt.

Why Lenders Make Bad Loans

Although with the help of computerized financial profiling lenders are getting a lot better at making good loans, they still make a fairly large number of bad ones.

TIP

A lender's "bad loan" can mean good profits for you.

To understand why lenders make bad loans, you must consider the plight of the lending officer. The most important officer in a lending institution is the one who makes loans, good loans. (A good loan is one which the borrower repays on time.) A lending officer who makes good loans can be highly rewarded.

The problem is that usually there is far more money to lend out than there are qualified borrowers for it. As a result, lending officers are caught between a rock and a hard place. If they produce the volume their employer wants, they are bound to get some bad loans. If they go only for good loans, they can't keep up the volume.

As a result, almost all lending institutions make some marginal loans and as a result, have some problems. (And the turnover rate for lending officers tends to be high!)

What Happens to Bad Mortgages?

Once a mortgage is nonperforming for a period of time and the borrower appears unable to correct the deficiencies (back interest payments and penalties), the lender will begin foreclosure.

TIP

Contrary to popular belief, most lenders do not start foreclosure when the first payment is late. Typically they will wait three to six months before beginning foreclosure proceedings, hoping the borrower will right the loan. Remember, they don't want the property back—they want a performing loan.

The loan is considered nonperforming throughout the foreclosure process. However, once the foreclosure is complete and the lender takes title to the property, the mortgage stops being nonperforming. It, in fact, stops being a mortgage at all. It is erased from the mortgage category and is instead placed on the books as a property valued at the amount of the mortgage. However, since the property generates no interest (lenders don't usually rent out their REOs), as noted, it becomes a liability.

As noted earlier, it doesn't take long for a lender to get into capital reserve troubles if it has too many REOs. Ten mortgages of $300,000 apiece converted to REOS tie up three million dollars of capital. It is to the lender's advantage, therefore, to get rid of that property as soon as possible. The lender wants to sell the REO and thus convert it back into either cash, which can be loaned out, or a new mortgage, which comes to the same thing.

The point is that lenders want to get rid of REOS in the worst way. They will go a long way to get rid of any they have, including making you a sweetheart deal on them. Thus, some of the best deals in a down market can be obtained by buying lender REOS.

Why Keep REOs Secret?

There is one stumbling block, however, to buying REOs from lenders. Almost universally, lenders won't admit publicly that they have an REO problem. Many won't admit they even have any REOs. Thus, you can't usually just walk in and ask to buy one.

This certainly seems to be working against a lender's best interests, at least on the surface. One would think that they would be out there advertising those properties as heavily as possible. Yet, they don't. Do you ever recall seeing a lender advertising under its own name for REO buyers? It normally just doesn't happen. (Most of the public isn't even familiar with the term "REO.")

The reasoning of the lenders is threefold:

First, a lender doesn't want to alert federal watchdogs that it has an REO problem. Keeping up a good face can mean the difference between remaining in business or being considered insolvent.

Second, depositors are wary about where they place their money. Yes, we know every account is guaranteed to $100,000. But, how many of us want to put that guarantee to the test? We might bolt if we thought the lender were shaky.

In addition, there are holders of amounts larger than $100,000 who frequently move funds from lender to lender trying to tie up the highest interest rates. These large depositors are not insured and will pull their funds at the slightest whiff of trouble from a lending institution. Hence, lenders are very careful not to admit they have many REOs, if for no other reason than to protect their own image.

Finally, there is the matter of the real estate market. If it got widely known that lenders had an overhang of homes ready to dump on the market in a particular area, it could adversely affect prices. This would backfire for the lenders since it would result in their receiving less money for the properties they are trying to sell.

Therefore, the lenders are close-mouthed about their REOs because:

1. They don't want to alert federal watchdogs.

2. They don't want to scare away depositors.

3. They don't want to hurt the real estate market.

How Do You Find Out About REOs?

All of the above reasons present a problem to you, as an investor, who wants to get an especially good deal in an REO. How do you find out about REOs when the lenders keep mum about them?

The truth is that while lenders keep quiet about REOs as far as the general public is concerned, they can be open about them to buyers. After all, they do want to sell them in order to get the money invested back at work as a mortgage.

You, as an investor therefore, have to convince the lender that you're a legitimate buyer. What you have to do to find REOs is tedious, but simple. It's tedious because you have to do it over and again for each lender, but otherwise the process is quite easy.

Basically you need to let a lender know that you are a sophisticated investor. You need to let the lender know that you understand what an REO is and that you'd like to bid on one.

Once the lender understands that you're special and not part of the public who are only interested in deposits, they will open up, at least in a limited way.

Finding REOs—An Example

I recently called up the main offices of a large lender in the San Jose, California, area. I asked to talk to the officer in charge of the REO department. For a few minutes the operator seem confused. They had a loan department, an escrow department, and an operations officer, but they didn't have an REO department listed.

I asked to talk to the operations officer. (The operations officer handles day-to-day operations of the lending institution.) I explained to her that I was an investor and wanted to speak to someone in the REO department. I was given a number to call.

When I called the number I explained that I was an investor interested in purchasing an REO. Could I get a list of REOs available from the lending institution?

No, I was told. No such list existed. (Hah! The lender didn't have a list of its own REOs? Come on now!)

I understood that I was just a voice on the other end of the line. I was someone unknown to the REO officer who wasn't about to release information considered delicate. So I tried a different ploy.

I said I was looking for REOs in a particular area. I gave the community, a rather small district of the city. Did the lender have any REOs in that area?

There was a pause, then the officer was saying that yes, there were three. If I was interested in them I could come down and fill out an identity form and they would then give me the addresses so I could go out and look them over.

Success!

As I said, it really isn't hard. But you have to do it for each lender and it's a little bit different each time.

Are REOs Listed?

Sometimes when you call a lender you will be told that all REOs are listed with local real estate agents. The agents handle the sale for the lender who has no direct sales to the public.

Fine. Deal with the agent.

I have bought REOs through agents and it works out okay. If the lender wants to pay a commission to a broker for handling the sale, it's no skin off my nose.

Typically a lender will designate a particular broker to handle all its REOs in an area. Usually it is one of the larger and more active offices.

After you find out who the agent is from the lender, just call up the office and ask to speak to "Jill Smith" who handles the REOs for "XYZ" lender. Usually there is one agent who does this, although in large offices sometimes all the agents "co-broke" or work on REO sales.

Talk to the agent. Explain that you're an investor looking for a good REO deal. Get to know the agent a bit and allow the agent to get to know you.

Typically you will be told that the agent doesn't have any REOs from the lender at the present time. The reason is quite simple. These are good deals and they sell quickly.

I can recall one REO I bought a few years ago in this manner from an agent. When told there were none available, I asked if any had recently been sold. Yes, I was told. One had, but it was in escrow.

Fine, I said. Could I see it?

Certainly. I was given the address and the agent later took me to the property. It was a nice house, run down, but in a good area and at a good price. I said I would like to make a "back up" offer on it. If the current offer fell through, I wanted mine to be considered.

Fine, said the agent, and wrote it up. My reasoning was quite simple. Most active investors, those who own lots of property, are spread thin. As a result, they often have little cash to put down or their income isn't sufficient to cover all their properties. In addition, over the years they may have lost one or two properties and the foreclosures show up on their credit reports. They may even be land poor, owning several valuable properties but unable to get their cash out. These active investors frequently know about REOs and often make offers which are accepted. But also frequently, these people don't qualify for financing, and the deal falls through.

This happened to be the case with me. The first buyer was rejected for a mortgage by the lender. My back-up offer, already written up, was submitted. And subsequently, I got the property.

No, it won't happen that way every time. But, it will happen that way enough to make it worthwhile trying.

Do I Have to Fix Up the REO?

REOs are often in distressed condition. Consider, if you were the borrower and were losing the house, your equity, and your credit rating, would you be anxious to keep watering the lawn or to clean up when you left?

Most borrowers who lose their property through foreclosure not only do not clean up, but actually go out of their way to mess up the property. Their reaction, naturally enough, is anger, and since they really can't take it out on anyone personally, they typically take it out on the property.

I have seen REOs where the sinks and toilets were ripped out, where all the windows were broken, where fecal material was rubbed into the carpets, where holes were smashed into the walls, and on and on. (I've often speculated that had the former owners spent half as much energy trying to make the payments as they did messing up the house, they might still own the property!)

When you get to the REO it may still be in terrible shape, or it may have been fixed up.

Lenders are no fools (although their lending policies sometimes suggest otherwise!). They know that a distressed property will get them a distressed price. On the other hand, if they fix it up even just cosmetically, they stand to get a far better price.

On the other hand, if you arrive on the spot just as the REO is acquired and offer to take it "as is," the lender may agree. After all, time spent fixing up the property is, once again, lost interest to the lender.

Thus, when you find an REO in distressed condition, don't turn your head away in disgust. You're not looking at a disaster, you may be looking at an opportunity.

How Do I Calculate Fix-Up and Clean-Up Costs?

Experienced investors can do this in just a few minutes. But, that's a result of their experience.

If you're new to the game, it's going to take you longer. If you find a distressed REO that otherwise fits your needs in terms of location, tenant market, etc. (see the next section), calculate the costs to fix it up.

You may have to call out a painter, plumber, and electrician. (In truth, to be successful, you're going to have to eventually make contact with "handymen" who can do this for you or you're going to have to learn how to do it yourself.) You may have to calculate the costs of having someone come in and clean out the mess. You'll have to calculate relandscaping costs and so forth. Here are some of the items you need to consider.

What to Consider When Refurbishing a Distressed Property

Clean Up (including washing kitchen appliances, such as stove and sink, and baths)

Carpeting and Pads (may need to be cleaned or replaced—watch out for pet urine in the carpet—often the smell cannot be removed and the carpet must be replaced)

Plumbing (including replacing fixtures such as baths, sinks, and toilets)

Electrical (putting in new light fixtures and repairing any damage)

Painting (inside and out where needed)

Landscaping (including new front lawn and garden—you can often get by without fixing up the back yard)

Fencing (often this is broken down and needs repair)

Roof (check for leaks which have to be fixed)

Plaster or Wall Board Repair (fix holes)

Doors and Door Handles (replace or repair)

Windows and Screens (replace)

Any Other Broken or Damaged Item

As you can see, the list is fairly long. It can also be fairly costly. It's important that you get as accurate a cost figure as possible. Remember, you'll be paying for it. Also, don't forget to include a figure for your time and effort, especially if you're going to be doing the work yourself.

TRAP

REOs are often in distressed neighborhoods. Remember to judge the neighborhood first and foremost. Don't become enraptured with dreams of refurbishing the house until you're convinced that the neighborhood warrants it. If there's a high crime and vandalism rate in the neighborhood, you may find that as quickly as you clean-up and fix-up, there's someone coming around to tear down and mess up. That's a hopeless situation, one of the worst, and you want to avoid it.

How Do I Make an Offer?

Once you've done your homework in determining that the REO is a good prospect in terms of location, rental market, etc. as outlined earlier, and you've determined the costs to bring it into rentable shape (unless you plan to flip it), you need to determine what you're going to offer the lender.

Keep in mind that everything in real estate, especially an REO, is negotiable. The lender may have set a price, but you don't have to pay it. You can make a lower offer or you can ask for favorable terms.

TIP

Good REO property is in high demand by investors. Keep in mind that there may be many offers on the house you are considering. The lender, naturally enough, is going to accept the best.

As a consequence, you need to make your offer as sweet as possible without hurting. I can recall one REO investor who beat me out on a house a few years back by offering nearly $10,000 more than I did. The lender, whom I knew fairly well, asked me if I wanted to raise my offer. I reexamined my figures and declined. I couldn't see a profit for me at the higher costs. So the lender gave the property to the other bidder.

As it turned out, she later admitted that she had overpaid and lost money on the deal. Remember, getting the property is only one battle. Winning the war means ultimately making a profit. If there's no profit, you're just spinning your wheels.

Offering All Cash to the Lender

The simplest offer (for the lender, not you) is to offer all cash. This doesn't mean that you need all cash—you can go out and secure financing on the property from a different lender. It just means that the lender is going to get all cash.

Typically how you arrive at a price for a cash deal is to calculate what the property is going to be worth when it's fixed up. Then work backward subtracting your realistic costs of fixing it up. (Don't forget to deduct interest payments during the fix-up period, as well as your own profit.)

The trouble with an all-cash offer is twofold. From the lender's perspective, it means selling for what might amount to a loss. From your perspective, it means going out and finding a separate, new lender who is willing to loan you money on a distressed property—not something always easy to find. There may be an easier way.

Can I Demand Terms?

Another way is to offer the lender terms. Offer a higher price for the property. In other words, you offer the current value of the home in its present condition, plus what it's worth when fixed up (but usually still less than market). However, you then request something like the following:

1. The lender will make you a 90 percent (or 100 percent, if possible) loan on the full purchase price at a favorable interest rate for a term of at least three years (based on a 30-year amortization). This allows you time to fix-up, rent, and hold until the market turns. It also guarantees that the lender will be out of the property for good after a set amount of time.

2. The lender will give you a "fix-up allowance" equal to your costs of refurbishing the property, all of which is to come out of the new loan. This simply means that the lender will give you cash back out of the new mortgage (typically made in payments as the work is completed) to fix up the property.

3. The lender will pay normal closing costs.

The above terms might appeal to a lender for several reasons. The first is the price. It can show that the property was sold at a better price than it might otherwise command and that it now has a, presumably, performing mortgage on it—an asset. In other words, there won't be a loss on the books.

Second, the lender doesn't have to go in and spend time and money fixing up the property itself; something which many lenders are ill-prepared to do.

Third, you are guaranteeing to fix up the property so that in the event that you don't make your payments and the lender has to re-foreclose, then the lender should be getting the property back in far better shape.

The above terms can be appealing to many lenders. Some lenders will take the offer, unless there is someone who's got a sharper pencil than you and offers more or asks for a lesser allowance.

What Are the Pitfalls in REOs?

It has been estimated that something approaching two-thirds of all REOs are distressed and that some of these are simply hopeless. If you're looking at distressed properties, it's important to determine which have possibilities and which are of the hopeless cast. The last thing you want to do is to relieve a lender of a hopeless problem and make it yours.

The important thing to remember is that the REO is most often sold "As Is," even if the lender refurbished it. The lender/seller makes no commitment to you of any kind. This can result in some bizarre problems.

No Disclosures

The lender may not give you any disclosures regarding the property. It may not be required to do so under state or federal law. Further, even if it does give you disclosures, they may be useless since it simply may not know what the problems with the property actually are.

Therefore, it's up to you to diligently inspect the property. The help of a good professional home inspector is invaluable here.

Cracked Slab—Case History

Jason bought an REO with a "cracked slab." In his area of the country, houses were typically built on slabs of concrete reinforced with steel instead of the more traditional peripheral foundation and raised wood floor.

Jason's house seemed alright to look at. However, it was on a slight hill and one side near the kitchen and dining room sank slightly where the slab was cracked.

Jason evaluated it carefully. He even called in a contractor to examine it. The conclusion was that the ground under the slab below the kitchen had moved outward slightly, causing the slab to fall. At the worst it was offset about three inches. The contractor said that to fix it "right" he'd have to rip down half the house and rebuild. Alternatively he could do a cosmetic fix. He figured he could just pour a new layer over the slab, lift up the walls, and the house would be ready to go.

A simple thing to correct, Jason thought. He made an offer on the REO based on the cosmetic change and was successful. A short time later, the house was his.

However, problems appeared as soon as he started refurbishing. It turned out that when the contractor began cutting out pieces of the old slab in order in order to blend in the new layer of concrete, he discovered that the reinforcing steel was missing. The original builder some 30 years earlier had failed to put it in!

Without steel, the cracked slab was free to move wherever it wanted. Putting a new layer of concrete on the top wouldn't help at all. The new layer would quickly crack, and perhaps sink, as the concrete continued to shift.

In addition the local building department showed up to ask why the contractor was working without a permit. (A neighbor had seen the work and complained.) The contractor immediately stopped work and applied for a permit, which was denied! The building department said that, given the lack of reinforcing steel, the only way it would allow work to proceed was to tear out the old cement (and half the house) and put in new cement and new steel.

This story does not have a happy ending. Jason complained to the lender. The lender said, "Sorry." Jason had signed an "As Is" clause. So Jason resold the property to a builder who did the refurbishing work correctly. However, Jason lost his original down payment and the money he'd spent refurbishing.

Bad Tenant—Case History

Jill bought an REO with a tenant in it. The tenant was there when she examined the property and claimed that he was paying rent to the lender.

Fine, Jill thought. Having a tenant already in place will save me some time and money. She went ahead with the purchase buying the property "As Is."

Once the deal went through, she went back and introduced herself as the new owner. She told the tenant that he should now pay the rent to her and she showed him the title papers. He slammed the door in her face, wouldn't let her in, and refused to talk to her.

As it turned out, he had been the tenant of the original owner who had rented out the property without living in it personally. When the property went into foreclosure, the tenant remained, not paying rent. He hadn't paid rent for the past five months and wasn't about to start now.

Jill tried to reason with him, but to no avail. So she secured the services of a real estate attorney who, for several thousand dollars and after a period of nine weeks, finally had the man evicted. During that time, of course, Jill couldn't fix up the property and she had to make mortgage payments and pay taxes and insurance.

TRAP

Beware of any REO that has anyone living in it. It could be a former tenant or a former owner. Regardless, NEVER take possession and close the deal until the property is vacant. Make it a condition of your purchase.

These two unfortunate scenarios are shown to let you see that REOs are not all peaches and cream. Problems can and do crop up for the unwary.

On the other hand, I and others have bought REOs successfully, the purchase has gone without incident, and they have been resold at a profit. Much, though not all, of the risk can be reduced by simply being careful.

9
Profit Strategy 5—Bargains in Government's Repos

The single biggest owner of residential real estate in the country is the federal government. This is not by choice, but mainly because of foreclosure. The government runs a host of programs which aid home buyers with financing. When those home buyers run into trouble and can't make their payments, ultimately it's the government that squares things with lenders and takes the homes back. Then it has the job of reselling them.

I know of several real estate investors who, over the years in good times and bad, have made a healthy living buying and reselling these government repos. Sometimes they are able to quickly flip these properties. Most times they simply buy, fix-up, and rent for a time and then resell (or refi or trade).

TRAP

Be careful of being too enthusiastic about flipping government repos. As of this writing there are several federal probes underway into investors who have made unconscionable profits at the expense of the government and rebuyers. The allegations are that investors, in collusion with lenders and appraisers, have bought the government repos at low cost and then artificially jacked up the prices to quickly resell to unqualified buyers at high prices for low or nothing down. When these rebuyers eventually can't make the payments, the government has to again foreclose on the same property. And that makes the government very unhappy and determined to quash those responsible.

The basic procedure for purchasing a government repo is fairly similar throughout various agencies. In most cases, but not all, you must purchase the home through a local real estate agent. (The government pays the agent's commission.) However, it's up to you to ferret out where the homes are and to determine if they are worth the investment.

TRAP

Just because it's a government repo doesn't automatically make it a bargain. The government tries to get as high a price as possible for these homes. Sometimes it asks market or even above!

In many cases the homes are in poor condition. That means that you must thoroughly investigate the property to determine what it will take to put it back into shape. (Check out the next chapter for clues on how to do this.) It's rare that you'll get a government repo in good shape at a good price. There are simply too many other people competing for these properties.

At the present time there are over a dozen different government programs that offer properties for sale. (See the list at the end of this chapter.) We're going to look at several of the biggest programs.

HUD Repos

The Housing and Urban Development Department takes back homes mainly through its FHA program. The FHA insures lenders who make loans. When a borrower defaults, the FHA makes good the loan to the lender, and takes the property back. At any given time it may have tens of thousands of repo'ed homes for sale across the country. You can check to see if there are any HUD homes in your area on the Internet at:

www.hud.gov/local/sams.ctznhome.html

Since the homes come back mainly through the FHA program and since that program has a maximum loan amount as of this writing of around $240,000, you're not likely to find many upscale properties here. Most are going to be in the moderate to low price range.

Additionally, they may not be in the best of condition. HUD usually does not fix up the properties. That means that they may be in anywhere from average to really bad shape. Don't be surprised at the terrible condition in which you may find a HUD home. Remember, the former owner lost the property to foreclosure. There was little incentive to keep it up. Additionally, since that time there may have been vandalism.

Making an Offer—As noted, you must make your offer through an agent who represents HUD in your local area. Once you locate a home that you're interested in, contact the referred agent and go see the property. The agent can arrange to have you walk through. You'll also make your offer directly through the agent.

Pricing—HUD tries to sell its homes at fair market price. However, sometimes this is difficult to determine because of the run-down condition of the property. Occasionally, particularly if you are sharp at knowing property values, you can find some real bargains here! (Check into the next chapter for tips on how to scout out run-down properties.)

Financing—HUD doesn't make loans directly, but it does work with lenders in a variety of programs. You may be able to get in with virtually nothing down, as long as you're intending to occupy the home. If you're buying as an investment, HUD will usually want at least 10 percent down. In other words, your financing needs here are going to be similar to those with any investment property. (Look into the next section for tips on getting investment loans.) HUD often looks with extra favor on buyers who submit offers that are a cash-out to HUD. In other words, buyers who get their own outside financing.

Owner-Occupants—As with many government programs, HUD aims to sell its homes to those who will occupy them. Read NOT to investors. Thus in the initial "offer period" those who intend to occupy the HUD homes are given priority in their offers. If you're looking for both a house to live in AND an investment, this can be the perfect choice for you.

Investors—However, if there are no owner-occupants who submit offers during the initial offer period, or the home does not sell in that time frame, then investors can make offers that will be considered.

Does this mean that you as an investor only have a chance at the leftovers? Not really. Remember, most of these homes are not in great shape and most owner-occupants are not eager to buy into them. Further, remember that HUD makes an effort to offer them at market price. For casual home owner-occupant buyers who don't really know the market, there may not seem like there are any bargains here.

As a result, very often these homes are sold to investors.

Fix-Up Allowance—If the home is in bad shape, HUD may offer a fix-up allowance. This can be either in the form of an additional price reduction, or a special fix-up loan. However, in order to get this, you must be sure it's part of your purchase offer. Once you've made your offer and it's accepted by HUD, it's too late to demand a fix-up allowance.

Bonuses—HUD may also offer special incentives, if it's particularly interested in moving a property. For owner-occupants this can include a moving allowance. For investors, this can include a bonus (price reduction) for closing the sale fast. If you have all your financing ducks in a row and can close within a week or two, it can make a significant financial difference.

Professional Inspection—To avoid buying a "pig in a poke" you'll want to have a professional inspection of the home. However, unlike conventional purchases where the professional inspection is normally conducted after you've signed a purchase agreement with the seller, with HUD you'll need to make your inspection beforehand. HUD doesn't like to tie up homes on contingencies that involve inspections.

As noted, at any given time there are thousands of HUD homes for sale in virtually every state. If you're interested in working the repo market, you owe it to yourself to check out the HUD program.

VA Repos

The Veteran's Administration has an extensive program of loan guarantees. Unlike HUD which *insures* loans to lenders, the VA *guar-*

antees the performance of a loan to a lender. (Actually, it guarantees only a small percentage of the top of the loan.) If the borrower defaults, the VA pays off its guaranteed portion. However, rather than simply pay out cash, the VA has determined that it is more profitable to actually buy the property from the lender who forecloses, and then resell it.

Initially only veterans who qualify (who were on active duty during specific time periods) can get VA loans in order to buy a home. After the VA has foreclosed, however, it opens the homes to anyone who wants to buy them, veteran or non-vet, investor or owner-occupant.

At the time of this writing the VA had over 21,000 homes for sale nationwide in its inventory and was averaging over nine months to sell them.

Making an Offer—To purchase a VA home, as with the HUD program, you must go through a local real estate agent who represents the VA's property management program. Typically these agents will advertise in local newspapers.

You may also find most, but not all, of them listed on the VA's property management website. Unlike HUD, the VA does not maintain an Internet presence with a list of all properties. It is up to the local property management office to determine whether to link to the VA website and whether to list its homes on the Web.

Check out:

www.homeloans.va.gov/homes.html

In order to make an actual offer, you must go through an agent and use the proper forms. These include the following:

Offer to Purchase/Contract of Sale (VA form 26-6705)

Credit Statement (VA form 26-6705B)

Financing—The VA will handle financing. However, it prefers to do this for owner-occupants. And it gives priority to buyers who come in with their own financing (cash to the VA). You'll usually, though not always, do better if you handle your own financing outside the VA.

Condition—As with HUD homes, many of the VA properties are in the same condition as when they were turned over after foreclosure. In the past, however, the VA has had an extensive program of refurbishing properties in order to get a higher market value. If you buy a refurbished home, don't expect to get any kind of bargain on the price. How the homes are handled is largely determined by the regional VA property management office.

Inspection—Again, you'll want to have a professional inspection so that you'll know what you're getting. However, as with HUD, you'll need to conduct the inspection during the offering period and not after you have your offer accepted. The agent who's handling the house can arrange for you and your inspector to get in. Be sure you use a sharp pencil when you calculate how much the property is really worth.

The VA program has been in existence for over 50 years. I've been involved with it at different times and in different ways and have seen many owners obtain solid investment property through it.

Fannie Mae Properties

Fannie Mae, along with Freddie Mac discussed next, is one of the main secondary lenders in the country. Together they underwrite most of the conventional (non-government insured or guaranteed) mortgages that are made. What this means is that when you get a mortgage from say, XYZ lender, it then in effect sells your mortgage to Fannie Mae or Freddie Mac, thereby receiving enough money to go out and make additional mortgages.

If, however, you fail to make your mortgage payments and fall into foreclosure, it's Fannie Mae or Freddie Mac (through whatever lender happens to be servicing the mortgage at the time) that takes the property back. Those agencies then have to get rid of it, similar to the way HUD or the VA must dispose of their properties. This again can present an opportunity for investors.

Property Types—Fannie Mae underwrites all types of single-family homes, including detached properties, condos, and townhomes. Most of their inventory consists of fairly new homes and often they are in modest to even upscale neighborhoods. My own observation is that the Fannie Mae properties tend to be a little classier than either the HUD or VA homes.

Property Location—As with HUD and the VA, Fannie Mae requires you to go through a local real estate agent. However, the agents are required to list all the homes on the local MLS, so there's no difficulty in gaining access. Any agent in the local board can show you the home, as well as make the offer for you. Your offer will then go to the listing agent who will in turn present it to Fannie Mae.

You can also find a list of Fannie Mae homes at the website:

www.fanniemae.com/homes.html

Making an Offer—The transaction is handled just as if you were dealing with any other conventional seller. Fannie Mae can accept, reject, or counter your offer. Indeed, you may go through several rounds of countering before the deal is finally done.

Unlike with either HUD or the VA, you can add contingencies and other conditions with your offer. You may demand to have a professional home inspection *after* the offer is accepted. You can also negotiate over terms, down payment, and financing. Fannie Mae will not, however, accept a contingency which first requires the sale of an existing home.

You may use your own title insurance and escrow company. However, usually in order to have your offer accepted, you must be pre-approved by a lender. That means that you've had your credit checked, and you've had income and cash on deposit verified.

Condition—These are repos, which means they may (or may not) be in poor condition. Sometimes Fannie Mae will fix up these properties in order to get a higher price. Sometimes they are left in the condition they were received. In any event, the homes are all sold in "As Is" condition, meaning the buyer must take them with whatever problems they have at the time of sale.

Financing—Fannie Mae does offer its own REO financing. However, it's typically not any better than you get elsewhere. Further, you may have a better chance of getting your offer accepted if you come in with cash to Fannie Mae (meaning, you secure outside financing).

As with other government repo programs, to get a bargain, you must be on top of the market. You must be able to recognize true value where others miss it. Making a sharp offer can often net you an excellent deal here.

Freddie Mac

As with Fannie Mae, Freddie Mac also offers single-family detached, condos, and townhomes. However, Freddie Mac generally cleans and fixes up its homes before offering them for sale. If you want to submit an offer on a home doing the fix-up work yourself, chances are Freddie Mac will still at least clean up the property before you buy it.

Through its HomeSteps program Freddie Mac will offer homes to owner-occupants at competitive interest rates with 5 percent low down payments and no mortgage insurance. It will also offset some of the title and escrow costs. These homes, however, are almost all competitively priced at market.

Freddie Mac homes are offered through a select group of lenders. To find out more about them, check into:

www.homesteps.com

Other Government Repo Programs

There are many other government repo programs, including some from the IRS as well as local government authorities. Here's a list you may find helpful in checking them out:

Customs: www.treas.gov/auctions.customs

Department of Veteran Affairs:
www.homeloans.va.gov/homes.htm

Federal Deposit Insurance Corporation:
www.fdic.gov/buying/owned/index.html

GSA: http://propertydisposal.gsa.gov/property/propforsale/

IRS: www.treas.gov/auctions/irs/real/html

Small Business Administration:
http://appl.sba.gov/pfsales/dsp_search.html

U.S. Marshals Service: www.usdoj.gov/marshals/assets/nsl.html

US Army Corps of Engineers:
www.sas.usace.army.mil/hapinv/haphomes.htm

TIP

You're best off checking these out at their websites. If you call, you could spend hours trying to reach the right person with the correct information. The websites, on the other hand, are generally organized to give you the information you need right away.

10

Profit Strategy 6— Hidden Treasures in Handyman Specials

There are many investors who make a handsome living doing nothing more than snooping around finding run-down properties, buying them at discount, fixing them up, and then reselling for a healthy profit. I've done it myself for many years. The best part of this is that it doesn't really matter what the market is like . . . you can profit in good times and bad.

Even more so than with other types of real estate, buying right here is critical. You can't pay more for the property than its cost plus the fix-up costs plus your markup. If you do, you won't be able to sell for a profit.

TRAP

The biggest mistake to make with a handyman special is to pay too much for the handyman special property. It's better to lose a deal or two, than to pay too much and end up having to sit on an over-expensive home.

Let's be sure we've got this straight. The cost of the property, plus the cost of the fix-up, plus your profits can't equal more than the ultimate market price. If they do, you won't be able to sell and get your money out.

TIP

With handyman specials it is possible to buy and rent. However, you usually put so much money, time, and effort into the property that you want to resell quickly to get your profits out. My own feeling is that you should not buy deep handyman specials if you want to rent. Just buy cosmetically challenged properties, do minimal fix-up, and rent these properties out.

How Do I Identify Good Handyman Specials?

At the onset it's important to understand that unlike most repos and REOs, handyman specials can be found in any market and in any neighborhood. You can find them in Beverly Hills. (I had a good friend who used to specialize in handyman specials in the best neighborhoods of Los Angeles, and who did quite well.)

Basically these are properties that the owners have let run down. It might be because of financial considerations, as in a foreclosure. But there might be other reasons as well. Divorce, death in the family, transfer—these and other reasons frequently lead owners to stop the upkeep on their properties.

Let a home go for a few months and the landscaping will look terrible. Let it go for a year or two, and paint and overall appearance will suffer. Abandon the property and let vandals get in and it will look like a bomb was set off inside. It doesn't take long for a property to skid downhill.

Of course, to paraphrase Shakespeare, "It's an ill wind that blows no man fortune." What you're looking for is the very eyesore that 99 percent of home buyers avoid. You want the house that looks bad, that has exhausted landscaping and paint, that's in terrible condition. You want it so you can buy it for less, fix it up, and sell for a profit.

Be Age Conscious

The most common kind of handyman specials, and the worst to purchase, are the older homes. I can remember once considering a handyman special in Piedmont, an exclusive area of Oakland, California. The house was priced at about two-thirds of the going market value for a house in that neighborhood in good condition. Naturally I was interested. However, what I saw made me turn away.

The house had been built around the turn of the century (the 19th century!). That meant that it had archaic heating, electrical, and plumbing systems. And they hadn't been much upgraded by previous owners. Of course, it didn't have air-conditioning. I estimated it would take tens of thousands of dollars to modernize the property so that it could be sold at top market value.

But the worst thing was not the obsolescence. It was the termites. The house was entirely wooden. And termites had gotten into the flooring. When you walked on the wooden floors they gave underneath your feet. Upon examination in the basement, I discovered that not only were the floor boards riddled with termite tunnels, but the joists and supporting beams were affected as well. When I mentioned this to the seller, she replied that she was willing to have the house thoroughly fumigated to get rid of the pests. Yes, fumigation would certainly do that. But what about existing damage to the wood?

TIP

Good information is the key to working the handyman special market. You need to know exactly what's wrong with the property and exactly how much it will take to fix it. If you don't know yourself, it's incumbent upon you to call in professionals who do know and can help you. Don't guess here. Bad guesses will cost you money.

My feeling was that this house was ready to fall down. To my way of thinking, it was a scraper worth just the value of the lot, which was considerably less than the asking price.

All of which is to say that the older the property, the more likely it is to have serious problems that will require costly repairs.

The ideal handyman special home will be under 20 years old. That means that virtually all of the problems are likely to be cosmetic—the easiest type to fix.

Be Wary of Identified Problems

Sometimes you'll locate a promising property only to be told by the seller (or the seller's agent) that it has a bit of a problem. "Nothing too serious, but something to be considered."

TIP

Always be double wary when someone tells you the problem isn't too serious. Assume then that it's VERY serious!

The two most common "nonserious" problems are a leaking roof and a cracked foundation. If someone identifies these problems in a house you are considering, what exactly are they talking about?

They are talking about money. A new roof costs about $10,000 to $20,000. A new foundation may start at about $25,000 and go up from there.

But, you may argue, can't a roof be patched and a crack in the foundation fixed?

Sometimes. But can you tell the difference? With roofs, very often the problem is that the materials have simply worn out. Fix one leak and you'll get three others. This is particularly the case with homes that have roofs over 20 years old. (Another common roofing problem can be bad flashing—problems with the metal that keeps the water out in the valleys, around chimneys, and other areas. Finding and fixing the leak can be tricky, though it's usually inexpensive.)

With foundations the biggest problem is ground slippage. The foundation is cracking because the underlying soil is giving way. This can be almost impossible to fix cheaply.

On the other hand, maybe it is just a simple leak or a simple foundation crack. If so, it could only cost a few hundred dollars to fix.

The problem is usually severe, however, when it's identified. If the seller or agent points out a shifting foundation or a leaky roof, just assume it's a big deal. If it weren't, chances are they wouldn't even bother to mention it.

Look for Cosmetic Specials

These are the rarest finds. But when one does turn up, it can be a gold mine. Usually what's happened is that there has been a death or divorce in the family. The property may or may not be lived in, but the person who normally would keep it up isn't around. And it has gone downhill.

You can tell a cosmetic fixer because it has certain identifiable features. These typically include the following:

Features Identifying a Cosmetic Special

1. Spots and stains on walls

2. Worn, frayed, stained carpeting

3. Broken windows and torn screens

4. Missing or grievously damaged appliances

5. Broken sinks, toilets, tubs, or showers

6. Damaged or broken-down fencing around property

7. Yellowed grass and dead landscaping around property

8. Doors off hinges (sometimes even the front door!)

9. Holes in yard (where someone tried to bury garbage)

10. Generally poor condition

After reading all of these features you may think I've misnamed the property. This sounds a lot more than cosmetic!

But it's not. All of the above can be fixed with a little money and a lot of attention. Spots and stains on walls and ceilings can be removed simply by repainting. Carpeting can be cleaned or replaced with inexpensive new carpeting. (Cheap new carpeting looks terrific, at least for awhile.)

Appliances, sinks, toilets, etc. can all be replaced relatively inexpensively. Doors can be rehung or fixed. Fencing can be straightened, and lawns and shrubs replanted. In short, for a few thousand dollars and some work, the house can be put back into shape.

Now, compare this to putting in a new foundation . . . or a new roof . . . or new electrical/plumbing/heating systems. You should quickly get the idea that a cosmetic fixer, if it's priced right, is indeed a golden nugget.

TIP

The whole point of finding a cosmetic fixer is to get a good house at a cheap buy. It LOOKS so bad that the price is driven down. On the other hand, houses with more serious problems often don't show it. They may be money pits, but they don't LOOK bad. Be careful.

Should I Offer Less?

When buying a handyman special, there's only one rule—offer less.

Offer much less than the seller is asking. I can almost guarantee that the seller thinks the house is worth more than it is worth. In fact, most sellers want full market price regardless of the condition of the property. Your biggest challenge will be to get them to think realistically and accept a reasonable offer.

Offer less than you think the property is worth. Unless you are very experienced in this field, chances are you will underestimate costs and time required to do work and overestimate what you can get for the fixed-up house. Therefore, after you get to your best estimate of what the work will cost, shave some off of that offer.

TIP

You can never go wrong in a handyman special by paying less. You can always go wrong by paying more.

Offer less in counter-offers. Chances are that after you make an offer for less on a handyman special, the seller will not accept, but instead will counter at a higher price (lower than asking, but higher than you offered).

The tendency at this point is to want to compromise. Okay, the seller's being reasonable and has come down. So why not be reasonable as well and come up? The reason is you'll end up paying too much. Offer less than you think you should on counter-offers. Yes, you'll miss an occasional good deal. But more often you'll avoid getting in over your head in an overpriced property.

Make the Offer Heavily Contingent

The trouble with buying handyman specials is getting all the information together in enough time to make an offer. If it's a hot property, you aren't going to be the only one out there bidding on it. So, you probably won't have time to get a plumber, roofer, electrician, soils engineer, and so forth out to give you an estimate of repairs and cost. (Indeed, you won't want to spend the bucks to get those people out until and unless you have some certainty that you'll get the property.)

So, make an offer, but make it contingent on your approving professional inspections. Give it your best shot in terms of price. But then, after you get the property tied up, eliminate the guess work by having the pros come in and tell you exactly what's involved and how much it will cost.

TIP

An inspection approval contingency allows you to back out of the deal (or negotiate for a lower price) if you don't approve an inspection report. Typically you have two weeks to conduct the inspections. If you don't like what they say, you're out of there. The only cost was your time and the fees of the inspectors. Be sure a competent agent or attorney draws up the contingency clause so you're fully protected.

Should I Give the Seller What He or She Wants?

Those who sell run-down properties are usually special sellers. They may be an executor or administrator of a will, a divorcee who wants money fast, or an out-of-state person who needs to unload the property. Determine the seller's needs (see Chapter 5) and then cater to the seller.

Perhaps the sellers need quick action. If you have already gotten your financing set, you may be able to offer them a three or even two week escrow. You'll buy for cash (to them) and they're out of there. That can mean a lot (in terms of a reduced price) to many people.

Or maybe your sellers are retirees who have the property paid off and want income at a good interest rate. Give them an assumable first mortgage at market. They'll love the income and may give you a price reduction to get it. And since the loan is assumable, you can have the rebuyer keep the loan when you sell. It benefits the original sellers, you, and the rebuyer (who won't have to pay points or expensive loan charges).

TIP

A mortgage at market can carry an interest rate almost twice as high as for a bank deposit. That's a big incentive for a seller with a lot of cash who wants income to go with the mortgage instead of the bank account.

What Work to Do and What Not to Do

Once you acquire the property, there's a fine line between work that will pay off, and work that means wasted time and money. Generally the rule is, do everything that shows. Do nothing that doesn't show.

Of course, in the real world, that's not possible. If the heating/air conditioning system is broken, you'll have to pay to get it fixed even though the cost will never show up. (The rebuyers will just assume that it's in working condition—they won't care a whit that you spent $2,000 to put it that way.)

On the other hand, there may be holes in the walls. Get them patched in a professional way. Give the wall a good coat of texture. And paint it with several coats of high quality paint. It won't cost that much, and it will show.

Similarly, don't hesitate to put new tile in the entrance way or to replace a badly worn front door. Both will show and will make a difference to a rebuyer.

Is There Any Special Financing for Handyman Specials?

Lenders won't always go along with your plans for a handyman special. They won't like the fact that the property is not in tip-top shape when you purchase it. They will want to lend you less.

That's not necessarily all bad. You can often make a deal with a lender to give you enough money up front to buy the property and then to give you money to fix it up. In this fashion the lender pays most if not all of your costs.

Will lenders do this? You won't know until you ask. Your best source for this type of financing are portfolio lenders. These are banks which keep their own loans (don't sell on the secondary market.) If you can demonstrate that you're a worthy borrower, they may make this special loan for you.

The government also offers similar loan programs. FHA Section 203(k) offers mortgage insurance to lenders (who actually make the loan) on homes that are at least a year old. The mortgage is given in two parts. The first part goes to pay the seller for the purchase. The second part is put into escrow until the property rehabilitation is completed.

These loans will work, particularly if you're living in the home and it's modestly priced. But the loans do have maximum and minimum limitations. You must also submit accurate cost estimates, architectural plans, and other documents, so there is some hassle involved.

However, the value of the mortgage is determined by the property value before rehabilitation plus costs to do the work, or 110 percent of the appraised value after rehabilitation (which ever works out to be less.)

Of course, there are always home equity loans and personal loans, even credit cards. A few investors I know purchase the property in the conventional way and then pay for the rehab work on credit cards!

When Should I Sell and for How Much?

We'll discuss selling in the fourth section of this book in detail. However, there are a few challenges specific to handyman specials that should be considered here.

First, as touched on earlier, should you rent or should you sell right after fixing up?

My own feeling is that it's usually better to sell a property that's been fixed up. For one thing, this gets me past the fixing up stage. Usually by the time the property's ready to go, I'm sick of working on it. If I rent it out, it means that it will continue to be there with calls from the tenants asking for repairs as they are needed.

Further, at the finish of fix-up time, the property will be in the best shape it's likely to be in for quite awhile. Should you use all that spit and polish to attract a tenant, or to attract a buyer? If you rent it out, keep in mind that you'll likely have to go through some refurbishing a second time, when the tenant does eventually move out, in order to make it ready to sell. So why not sell now?

Of course, a lot depends on the market condition. If the market is down, you may well want to hang onto the property for a time until things turn around. Renting, then, would make good sense. On the other hand, if the market's up, then you should be able to get a good price . . . and get out.

If you've done your homework and bought low and kept your rehab expenses in check, you should now be able sell for a healthy profit.

11
Profit Strategy 7— Finding Bargains on the Internet

It's been said that 85 percent of all properties for sale are listed on the Internet. I think that figure is wrong. It's closer to 95 percent!

Many sellers don't even know their properties are so listed. For example, very often when a seller lists with an agent who puts the property on the MLS (Multiple Listing Service), it also is listed on www.realtor.com, the site of the National Association of Realtors®, which usually has more than a million listings at any given time.

Then there are the dozens of FSBO (For Sale By Owner) listing sites which carry properties not listed by agents, but offered for sale directly by the seller.

All of which is to say that if you're a savvy real estate investor, in today's world you can scout out bargain properties without even leaving your home. You can do it from your computer by checking the Internet listings!

Can You Buy an Investment House Off the Internet?

It's important to understand the advantages and the limitations of searching for bargain property on the Web. The advantages include the following:

- Easily viewed listings of almost all houses that are available
- Color pictures of the homes as well as (sometimes) virtual tours

- Textual descriptions including lot and house size, number of bedrooms and baths, and so on
- Location of the property, often including a map showing how to get there
- E-mail and phone address of the seller and/or agent (You can communicate with them directly by E-mail)

From the above it should be obvious that you can very quickly scan dozens if not hundreds of listings from the comfort of your computer room. This tends to be far more efficient than trying to look at a listing book in an agent's office. It's certainly more efficient than touring streets hunting for FSBO signs.

On the other hand, once you find a listing you are interested in, it again becomes a physical game. The disadvantages of the Internet include:

- You cannot actually see the property or neighborhood. You must view it by physically going to it, which is critically important.
- As of this writing you cannot easily make binding offers over the Web. At least one website, www.eStreetRealty.com, was allowing you to offer and/or bid on properties over the Internet, but successful offers must be followed up by a physical contract.
- You should physically go with any professional conducting an inspection of the property, to learn firsthand of any problems or defects.

Thus, the Internet is basically a happy hunting ground. It allows you to more easily locate properties that you might want to invest in.

How Do I Recognize a Bargain?

That, of course, is the rub. The listings on the Internet can tell you loads of information about any given property. But, they can't tell you if it's a good buy.

TIP

Sometimes listings can be helpful. For example, if they say that the owner is very anxious to sell, you may surmise that you've got a highly motivated seller.

To discern a good buy, you must do your own homework. This is the reason that I suggest you learn to "farm" an area.

What Is "Farming for Bargains"?

"Farming" is a term used by real estate agents to refer to a process of soliciting listings. It simply means that the agent will pick a neighborhood or group of neighborhoods close to home and then go door-to-door planting seeds by introducing him or herself as a broker or salesperson in the area. If the owners ever need to sell their homes, the agent is available.

Planting is followed by fertilization, when the agent regularly sends cards and flyers describing area homes that are for sale and area homes that were sold.

Watering is when the agent attends neighborhood picnics, softball games, street fairs, and so on.

The entire process is called farming. The hope is that when an owner eventually wants to sell, he or she will turn to this "farmer" for the listing.

You can do the same thing, sort of. Of course, you're not looking for listings, but for properties to purchase. A determined investor will actually do the whole process from going door-to-door to let people know he or she is interested in buying, to sending out flyers, to attending neighborhood events.

You don't have to farm that thoroughly. Rather, you can simply tour the neighborhoods you've designated, checking out all the properties that are for sale and tracking the price of those sold.

TIP

It only takes one day a month to track For Sale and Sold homes in neighborhoods. Yet, that one day will bring you up to speed on market values.

I always suggest picking neighborhoods close to home, so it won't take long to track. You can actually cover several square miles of land that way in a short time.

The payoff for this exercise is that when you see a home newly listed on the Internet that's in your farm area, you will immediately know the following:

- Whether the home is priced high, average, or is a bargain
- Where the home is (roughly) and what the neighborhood is like
- Whether it's something you would be interested in

By being up on nearby neighborhoods, you know as much (sometimes more) than agents. Also, you don't need to spend days trying to decide if it's a good deal or not. You have a sense of it immediately, meaning you can act before someone else beats you out.

Can I Use Internet Services?

Of course, you will want confirmation of your first judgments. You will want to be sure about comparable sales in the area to confirm market value.

And if you buy you will need to get a professional inspector to check out the property, a title and escrow company to handle the closing, and other services. All of these are available over the Internet. You can find websites for:

Comparables sold in the neighborhood

Information on schools and crime in the area

Home inspectors

Title reports

Foreclosures

It's simply a matter of locating a website that caters to what you need. A few service websites that I have found helpful in terms of providing investor services include:

www.dataquick.com

www.monsterdata.com

www.eStreetRealty.com

Are the Listing Sites Really Worthwhile?

Actually, my favorite hunting grounds are the many FSBO sites, although I do look through the agent listings on www.realtor.com as well. As I said, the key to success comes in knowing the area better than the agents or the lister/sellers. In other words, when you see a bargain, you need to be able to realize it.

Not long ago I bought a house that was listed by an agent on the Internet. The listing included the usual picture of the property as well as its vital statistics. The price was about average for the area, which I knew well. However, what I paid particular attention to was a comment that the seller was very anxious to sell.

TIP

The Internet is international. That means that it doesn't discriminate in terms of locales. Listings can be for anywhere in the country (or the world). You have to be very careful to scout out those properties that are located near you—in your farm area—where you have the most knowledge of the market.

The listing mentioned above indicated that the price had been dropped significantly. So, I sent an E-mail to the agent asking just how desperate the seller was.

The agent immediately wrote back saying the seller was now a transfer company. The original sellers had tried unsuccessfully to unload the property and then an employer had hired a transfer company to handle the transaction. The transfer company now had title and was anxious to get rid of it. It was lowering the price $10,000 a week to dump it! The price when I called, in fact, was $30,000 less than that shown on the e-Listing.

Naturally I was interested. I immediately confirmed the price as being a bargain per comparables on a website, and made an appointment to see the property the next day.

TRAP

While the Internet provides all sorts of virtual opportunities in real estate, nothing takes the place of physically examining the property. Virtual tours are okay, but don't rely on them when making a purchase.

It was a single-family home in a very good upscale location. However, it was around 25 years old and it had not been renovated. That meant that it had the original kitchen and bathrooms—read old fashioned. In order to get top dollar, the house would require some renovation.

I had already secured my own financing (see the next section) so I was ready to go. I offered to purchase for cash to the seller (my financing, of course), at the current asking price less $25,000, the amount it would take by my estimates to do minor renovations to the kitchen and bathroom to bring them up to modern standards.

The agent submitted the offer and the transfer company countered at their then current price. The agent said they wouldn't come down a dollar.

I pointed out they were already dropping the price $10,000 a week in the hope of finding a buyer. Why not negotiate now over price?

The agent couldn't say. The transfer company's reasons were a mystery.

So I waited two weeks. Of course, I was on pins and needles worrying that someone else would slip in and buy the property. But, apparently the outdated kitchen and baths were a real detraction in the home's higher price range.

Then, I submitted my offer again. This time I was only $5,000 off the asking price. The transfer company countered by dropping their price $2,500. I held firm. They capitulated, and I had the house. I'm now in the process of fixing it up and then plan to resell it. Prices have gone up in the area, as have my anticipated profits.

Of course, I might have found the house by checking local listings. The property was listed locally. But, looking at local listing books isn't really as informative, in some ways, as seeing the property on the Web along with color pictures. And then there are all those properties that aren't listed with agents that very well might be listed on the Internet.

What About Bargains in FSBOs?

A friend of mine recently had a good experience finding a house that was listed by its owner on a FSBO website. Similarly, he saw the price and the picture, and it sparked his interest.

TIP

Not all that many people scan the FSBO sites. This means that the competition for homes here is not nearly as tight as you might guess. Oftentimes bargains simply go begging.

Buying from an owner, however, is not the same as buying through an agent. What is missing is the buffer between the buyer and seller that the agent provides.

Tony found that while the seller was happy to show off the property, he kept pointing out all the little touches that he had added. After awhile it became apparent that the seller had so much of a personal interest in the property that he would have trouble seeing the sale as a business proposition.

Nevertheless, Tony gave the seller an offer substantially below the asking price, which was itself slightly below market.

The seller hemmed and hawed and said he couldn't go anywhere near that low. Tony pointed out that the seller was saving the real estate commission (5 to 7 percent in the area) and easily could go that low. But, the seller had pointed out, he had intended on keeping that commission for himself, or else why bother to sell FSBO!

In the end, Tony simply had to be blunt. Did the seller want to sell or not, for the price and terms being offered? The seller capitulated and a deal was made.

It was a successful conclusion, all of which began when Tony located the house on the Internet.

Popular FSBO Listing Sites

www.owners.com

www.homebytes.com

www.ehomes.com

12

Profit Strategy 8—Convert Your Old House to a Rental When You Move

If you're considering selling and moving up (or down), you may already own the perfect investment property, your current home!

Most people sell their current house when they buy another. They only own one home at a time. But, if your investment goal is to come up with an investment property, why not convert your existing home to a rental when you buy your next home to live in?

Is Conversion a Good Idea?

Keep in mind that you must want to sell your present home for this scenario to work. After all, you have to live somewhere! However, if this is something that's already in the works, then consider how a conversion could offer benefits.

There are all sorts of good reasons for doing a conversion. The biggest, however, are that you already know the property and own it. You don't have to go through the process of finding, investigating, and buying. It's a done deal right away.

But, many owners will immediately protest that they need the equity from their current home in order to buy their next one.

Not necessarily. You may be able to swing the deal with little financial strain, if you know how. We'll look into equity conversion shortly.

But first, how do you know if your home would make a good rental property?

TRAP

Not all homes make good investment property. You should do an analysis of your home before making the decision to keep and rent it.

When deciding whether or not your home would make a good investment property that you could rent out for awhile, consider all of the following:

1. **Is your home a suitable rental?** Not all properties are. Some simply require too much loving tender care. These are typically homes with extensive landscaping, with white carpeting, with delicate nooks and crannies . . . a high maintenance property. If you have one of these, you're probably better off selling. The home needs the care of an owner, which is not something a tenant will provide.

2. **Is your home in a good rental area?** Some areas are near large employers and for that reason, have a ready-made rental base. Others are in the far suburbs where there are almost exclusively home owners. Check out the rental market in your area. Look in the local newspapers. Are there lots of rentals? If so, do they rent up quickly? To learn quickly, call a few landlords and agents.

3. **Do you have rules restricting rentals?** Some properties have HOAs (Home Owner Associations) or Boards that want approval of renters. This is particularly the case with co-ops. Some single-family homes are in an HOA (often a gated community) and they show their disdain of rental properties by continually fining owner/landlords for rule infractions. If you have an HOA or a Board, it's worth taking a little time to find out just what their policy is toward rentals.

4. **Can you make more by selling outright?** Sometimes it makes more sense to sell than to rent. If you're at the peak of the market cycle, you might want to get out while the getting is good. On the other hand, if you anticipate much higher prices in the near future, you're far better off to hold for a time.

5. **Are you willing to be a landlord?** We've mentioned this else-where, but the truth of the matter is that if you convert, you'll be the one to go out there collecting rent, fixing faucets, and getting calls when you least want them. Be sure you're ready for this!

If your home makes muster, then by all means consider convert-ing to a rental and holding for a time to get a better price. You'll become an instant investor!

How Do I Handle the Equity Conversion?

This is the most frequently voiced concern when converting the old house to a rental property. You've got all your money tied up in your home's equity. You believe you need to get it out in order to buy your next home. So how can you convert?

There are many answers and we'll consider several:

Refinance—Before you sell your existing home, you can refi-nance it. This is an excellent time to do so because lenders will normally give you up to 95 percent of the market value. The rea-son they're so generous is because you're an owner-occupant. If it was an investment property, they might be less generous and cut down on the LTV (Loan To Value) ratio. You then take the money from the refi and use it to purchase your next home.

TIP

It's a good idea to refi well in advance of your next pur-chase (at least six months). This will help to keep your credit from being strained.

Low-Down—When you buy your next home, you simply don't put much money down. As we'll see in the next section, if you're buying property to live in, mortgages with as little as 3 percent down are available. You may have enough in savings to easily cover that amount. Thus, you simply leave your equity in the old property.

Savings—Finally, if available, you can use money from savings, from cashing in bonds or stocks, or from other sources to help you get into your new home. Remember, the money is not being thrown away. It's simply being converted from one investment venue to another.

How Do I Handle Two Monthly Payments?

Again, a big concern for novice investors. You'll have to make the mortgage payment on both your existing home, now converted to a rental, and on the new home that you're buying. That's two payments instead of one. And you're pretty sure that your income won't stretch that far.

Of course, this is always the dilemma of investors in real estate. If you went out and bought a rental property, you'd also have two payments.

Keep in mind, however, that you now have rental income. Income, after all, is the whole purpose of renting out real estate. And that rental income, if you selected the property wisely, should be enough to cover at least one of your payments.

For example, if you refi'd your old home, the payments would be higher. But, hopefully, the rental income would cover them.

On the other hand, if you went low-down on your new house, your new payments would be higher. But, hopefully, the rental income from the old house would be enough to cover your old payments as well as leave some left over to help with your new payments.

TIP

If you leave your equity in your old property, you may have a low enough existing mortgage that rental income will be higher than your monthly payments. This can offset high payments elsewhere.

Of course, there is always the matter of risk. Your rental property (old home) could be vacant for awhile before you find a suitable tenant. Or you could be unlucky and get a bad tenant who needs to be evicted and you lose some rental income there. (We'll discuss how to deal with such things in Part 3 on landlording.)

Those are a few of the risks of investing in real estate. And they're a good reason why it's important to hold some money back in reserve. However, as with all investments, you must measure the rewards. Is it worthwhile to assume risk to get the profits available? If you're answer is yes, then you may want to move forward with your conversion.

Are There Any Tax Consequences of Converting?

NOTE: The following discussion is not designed to give tax advice, but simply to give an overview of a few real estate tax rules. Consult with a professional if you desire tax advice.

Not immediately. After all, you're not selling your old home. You're just renting it out. So, until it comes time to file your next tax returns, there shouldn't be any consequences. But, there will be when you do file those returns . . . and when you eventually sell the property.

The tax rules with regard to handling rental properties are a bit arcane. There may be some benefits. Depreciation, for example, could give you a paper loss. This might be deducted from your other ordinary income IF your income is below a certain threshold. We'll have more to say about this in Chapter 20.

However, one benefit that you will lose when you convert to a rental is the ability to exclude the gain on your home. Under current tax rules, an individual who sells a *principal residence* can exclude up to $250,000 of the capital gain on the sale (up to $500,000 for a married couple). While there are other conditions that must be met, including a two-out-of-five year residence requirement, the part of the rule we're concerned with here is that the property must be your main home. It can't be both your main home AND a rental property. It's either one or the other. And if it's a rental property, you lose the exclusion benefit.

TIP

If you have a multiple-family building (such as a duplex, triplex, or small apartments), you may be able to live in one unit and rent the others out. When that's the case, the portion in which you live may have the exclusion available, while the portion rented out may not.

Thus, you may lose some tax benefits when you convert to a rental. Or not. As I said, the rules are a bit arcane.

As noted, the residency is two-out-of-five years. To qualify for the exclusion, you must live in your property for at least two years. However, it can be any two years out of five.

For example, you could live in your existing home for two years, then rent it out for the next three. When you sell, presumably, you could qualify for the exclusion because you had previously lived in it for two years within the time frame.

OR, you could have lived in it for only one year. Then you could rent it out for three years and move back in for a year, at which time you'd again qualify for the exclusion.

Thus, converting your home to a rental does not necessarily, or at least immediately, remove you from receiving the benefits of the up to $250,000 exclusion.

Furthermore, you can be building up time toward the two years in your new home. If you play the timing right, you could theoretically get the benefit of the exclusion in both properties. (Be sure to see your accountant before attempting this.)

Exchanging

Yet another tool available to you if you have a rental is the tax-deferred exchange. We'll have more to say about this in Chapter 20, but suffice to say for now that it allows you to sell and buy a new property while deferring any payment of tax in the transfer.

How Do I Get Started?

Your first move should be to get yourself preapproved by a lender. This will let you know the maximum mortgage and monthly payment you can get on your next home.

Preapproval

Once you know the maximum mortgage and monthly payment, you can proceed to make a decision regarding the equity in your property. For example, if you can qualify for a big enough loan, you may want to leave the equity in your existing property in place and simply buy the new home outright.

On the other hand, if you can't get a big enough loan on the new home, you may want to refi your old one to get your cash out. And then, after an appropriate period of time, you will want to proceed with the purchase of a new home.

Find Your New Home

Suddenly your task changes. Instead of looking for investment property, as discussed in this book thus far, you're looking for a home to live in—a different story. (Remember, you already have the investment property—your existing home!)

Now you can indulge yourself. You can look for things that you like, rather than things a tenant might like.

TIP

Remember, you will eventually want to resell any property that you buy. Therefore, buying with an eye toward a future buyer only makes common sense.

Make the Purchase

It should be a straight purchase for the new home. You won't need to make it contingent upon the sale of your old home, because you're not selling it. Just as you won't need to wait for the sale to purchase the new one. This should help you to negotiate a better deal on your new property. (Contingencies tend to get you a reduced price.)

Do the Conversion

As soon as the purchase of your new home goes through and you move in, you'll want to rent up your old home. You can try to rent your old home even before you leave. Put an ad in the newspaper and see what happens. But be prepared to have prospective tenants bothering you day and night to see the property. (It's just as bad as having to always have the place fixed up and ready to show to prospective buyers!)

Whether or not it's already rented, however, once you move out, be prepared to fix up the old house. Even though it may look clean while you're living in it, at minimum you should do the following:

- Clean the carpets
- Paint any rooms that have scratches or marks on the walls
- Have the kitchen and bathrooms professionally cleaned
- Be sure all appliances are working
- Get all your stuff out!

TIP

If you offer a clean home, you're likely to secure a clean tenant.

Perhaps the biggest mistake that those converting old homes to rentals make is to leave some of their old stuff in the rental home. After all, when you move you tend to get overwhelmed by the amount of stuff you've accumulated. Wouldn't it be simple to just leave a lot of it at the old place?

That won't work. Tenants expect to use the entire home, including garage and storage areas. You'll have to get all of your things out BEFORE the tenant can move in.

We'll have more to say about renting to good tenants and collecting rents in Part 3. For now, however, just consider a conversion. It can be the quickest and easiest way to acquire a good investment property.

Part 2

Multiply Your Cash

13

How to Get an Investment Mortgage

Not that many years ago the biggest problem with investing in real estate was getting financing. Institutional lenders (read banks, savings and loans, and so forth) were loath to lend money to people who wanted to invest. The thinking was that the money would be at high risk. If times turned bad, or if the investor made a mistake, he or she would simply walk away from the property leaving the lender to take the fall.

As a result, lenders limited their liability by insisting that investors put up more money. At a time when owner-occupant borrowers were getting 95 percent loans, the maximum investors could get would be 75 percent loans. That means on a $200,000 house, an owner-occupant only need put up $10,000. But an investor buying the same property had to come up with $50,000!

Needless to say this didn't encourage investing in residential real estate!

TIP

It did, however, encourage lying. Many would-be investors would claim that they intended to live in the property in order to get the better financing, then they would simply never move in, but rent the home out instead. This resulted in a kind of cat-and-mouse game where lenders would use such techniques as sending the mortgage payment book marked "do not forward" to the subject house, or lenders would call after 30 days to be sure the borrower was indeed living on the premises. In times past the penalties for lying were rarely enforced, and, unless the investor did it repeatedly, I don't recall many getting caught.

What About Investor 90-Percent Mortgages?

That all changed a few years ago with the introduction of mortgage computer-profiling, in which computers create a financial profile of a successful borrower (and an unsuccessful borrower). By comparing a borrower's credit history to an existing financial profile, lenders discovered they could much more accurately determine who would make the payments, and who would default and let the property go into foreclosure.

At first this financial profiling was done exclusively for owner-occupants. But more recently it has been used for investors. As a result, it is now possible to get much better financing on property you want to buy for investment.

The current standard investment mortgage is 90 percent LTV (Loan To Value). On a $200,000 house the investor must come up with only $20,000. That's less than half of the previous down payment requirement.

However, even though the new financial profiling system allows lenders to zero in on good payers, they are still loath to give up the old system. Hence, there remains a small interest rate penalty for investors. If you buy to invest, you'll pay a slightly higher interest rate. This is expressed in points.

Recently, when the interest rate *without points* for an owner-occupant was 8 percent, the interest rate *with points* for an investor was as follows:

Extra Points an Investor Must Pay to Get Mortgage

Loan To Value	Points[*]
75%	1.5
80%	2.0
90%	2.5

*The amount varies at different times.

As those who are in real estate know, "points" are interest prepaid at the time the mortgage is given. One point is equal to one percent of a mortgage. For example, one point on a $100,000 mortgage is $1,000. If you have 2.5 points and are borrowing $200,000 that means you must come up with $5,000. (In actual practice the loan amount is reduced by $5,000—you pay back $200,000, but only receive $195,000.)

Points add to the lender's effective interest rate. In the above example, if the lender only loans $195,000 but the borrower must pay back $200,000 at, for example, 8 percent, the yield to the lender is actually about 8.375 percent.

TIP

You can avoid paying points by agreeing up front to pay a higher interest rate. In the above example, if the investor-borrower agreed to pay an interest rate of 8.375 percent, then there would be no points. Points are simply another way of increasing the yield—getting more interest—for the lender.

While this may seem arcane, it's actually quite simple. To avoid any confusion, just remember that it costs investors a bit more interest to get the same mortgage than it costs owner-occupants.

However, even as of this writing it is not generally possible for investors to get mortgages for higher than 90 percent. This is at the same time as owner-occupants can get mortgages for as little as 3 percent down.

While there are no "no-down" or "super low-down" institutional investor mortgages, that still doesn't mean that you can't buy an investment property with nothing down, as we'll see in the next chapter.

TRAP

Some investors will still claim that they intend to live in the property in order to get the slightly lower interest rate and significantly lower down payment offered to owner-occupants. Be forewarned, however, that almost all institutional mortgages are government insured, guaranteed, or repurchased. All of which means that if you're caught, you'll have to answer to the Treasury Department.

How Do I Qualify for an Investment Mortgage?

We've already said that getting an investor mortgage involves the same financial profiling system used to qualify owner-occupants. It has to do with how credit-worthy you are.

However, there's an additional wrinkle if you intend to buy and rent out the property. There's the matter of having enough income to support the mortgage, according to how lenders calculate such matters. Thus there are two ways that you must qualify: the profile and your income.

Financial Profile Qualifying

The financial profile system works in this manner. In order to get a mortgage, you are given a three-bureau credit check. That checks out your credit with the three national credit checking bureaus: Equifax, TransUnion, and Experion.

This produces a raw credit report, which you may receive if you request it. It will show late payments, bankruptcies, foreclosures, and so on. (Interestingly, it sometimes will NOT show if you are paying your current mortgage on time—I suspect mortgage lenders don't like to let other lenders know who the really good payers are for fear of losing them!)

That raw data is then interpreted by sending it into a computer that compares it to other borrowers, both those who have been successful and those who have defaulted on their loans. This is called financial profiling. Fannie Mae and Freddie Mac, the two national secondary lenders, use their own system, as well as relying on FICO (Fair Isaac), a private system used extensively to financially profile borrowers. And the credit bureaus have their own "bankruptcy rating" or other financial profiling systems as well.

All of these systems take into account your credit habits. For example, if you apply for credit more than three times within a six-month period using the FICO system, it could have an adverse affect on your rating. (Too many applications suggest that you may be desperate to get money.) Having a large existing mortgage and high borrowing levels on credit cards could adversely affect you in another system (implying that you're in over your head.) And so on.

You usually will be told your rating. For example, anything over 700 on FICO is usually considered a top credit risk. But, in the past you were rarely allowed to see the actual reasons for your rating. Most rating systems preferred that the way they do their work be kept under wraps. Their fear was that if consumers (investors in this case) understood how the system worked, they would change their credit habits to get a better rating. Recent threats of federal legislation requiring better disclosure have led to an opening up of FICO and other rating systems. By the time you read this you may be able to get more detailed information on why your credit rating is what it is.

TIP

The trouble with the credit profiling systems is that they don't allow for exceptions. For example, you may have been car shopping and in a single day had credit checks from half a dozen dealers. Ultimately, you may not have even bought a car or gotten a car loan. But the checks may still appear, and could adversely affect your credit. There's really no efficient way to explain, "Hey, I was just car shopping!"

Suffice to say that in order to get the best investor mortgage, you'll need a high credit score. However, getting a lower score will not necessarily eliminate you from a mortgage. It may just mean that you'll pay more points (pay a higher interest rate) to get the same loan.

Income Qualifying

In addition, to be credit-worthy enough to get an institutional investor loan, as described above, you must also have enough outside income. That means that you must make enough money to support the investment.

But, you may argue, the investment is going to support itself. If I buy a rental house, the rental income will pay for PITI (Principle, Interest, Mortgage, and Insurance). That's better than an owner-occupant who will get no income from the property.

So you say. But lenders say otherwise. They want you to qualify for the investment property just as if it were a property you intended to occupy. And that gets a little bit difficult.

The reason is that you already are living somewhere and are paying rent or mortgage payments. Now, when you want to buy an investment property and get an investment loan, your home payments become an expense. If the basic qualifying formula is that income must be three times payments (the actual formula is close to this), that means you need to earn much more income to qualify for the investment mortgage.

Not sure why? Let's go over it in a bit more detail.

Let's say your own home mortgage is $1,000 a month. To qualify for it at three times, you need roughly $3,000 a month.

Now let's say you want to buy a rental property with PITI of also $1,000 a month. Again, you need $3,000 a month income. But, you no longer have $3,000 a month income because $1,000 of it got subtracted to pay for your home mortgage. Now you need $4,000 a month income to qualify!

But, you may still be arguing, the rental property produces $800 a month in income ($200 negative), so that gets added in and you're almost back where you started. Ah, if things were only so logical.

Lenders will take into account your rental income, but not all of it. They'll only allow 75 percent, in this case $600. They figure the other 25 percent will be lost to vacancies, maintenance, and other expenses.

Further, they'll only allow that $600 to be added to your income, not subtracted from your expenses. Thus, in our example where you need $4,000 to qualify, the lenders will subtract that $600 (75 percent of rental income) from the outside income you need to qualify. Now, instead of $4,000 you need $3,400 to qualify.

Got it?!

If not, just keep in mind that in order to get an institutional investment mortgage, you need more income than you need to qualify for an owner-occupant mortgage. Further, the more investment homes you own, the harder it becomes to buy the next one. Each time you need more income to qualify for the next loan!

TIP

Once again, that's another reason that many investors lie about their intentions when buying an investment home, and say they intend to occupy the property when they really don't.

What About Buying to Convert?

While I've made a big thing about being careful not to lie to a lender about your intentions (not to claim that you intend to occupy the property when you really don't), what if you really do intend to occupy the property?

If you plan to occupy the property, you get a lower down payment (as low as 3 percent), a lower interest rate, and easier income qualifying. That's a big incentive to move in. So why not do it?

I've known many investors who over the years have moved regularly from one property to another. They buy, move in, live there for awhile, and then convert to a rental. There's no law I know of against it.

The question for many, however, becomes one of how long do you need to live in the property to prove that you really intended to occupy it? I don't know the answer to that. Some people say as little as three months. Others say a year. (Some say it's impossible to prove intent and simply never move in—I suspect you might get away with that argument once, but do it over and again and someone's going to pull the rug out from under.) It's something you need to check out with your accountant, lawyer, and conscience.

What About Financing a Flipped Property?

How do you finance a property you intend to flip? Do you need to finance it?

In Chapter 3 we discussed the possibility of flipping a property right in escrow so that you never actually take title. Obviously, in that scenario there's no need for financing.

However, if you do take title and then quickly resell, say in a month or so, how do you handle the financing?

My suggestion is that if you're sure that you're going to flip the property and not keep it as a rental, go with any financing you can get. The easiest will probably be some sort of bridge loan (discussed below). If, on the other hand, you want to play it safe and aren't sure you can flip the property, then get long-term financing as discussed above.

A bridge loan came into existence to help home owners purchase a new home while they still had not sold their old home. The loan bridged the gap between the two properties. (Which is why it is sometimes called gap financing.)

A bridge loan allowed the borrower to buy the new property and hold onto it for six months or so until the older property sold. Then, in one scenario, a permanent loan was taken out on the new home.

For our purposes, bridge financing means any short-term (six months or less) loan, even a personal loan, that allows us to complete the purchase of the investment property. We don't need a long-term permanent loan because we intend to flip the home.

These short-term loans are available mainly from commercial banks. Typically they will tie up the property as well as your personal assets (in other words, everything in sight!). They are sometimes at a comparatively high interest rate (or, if you put up other assets, at a comparatively low interest rate, as discussed below).

However, on the other hand, they may actually be easier to qualify for. And if you have substantial assets in the bank (a savings account, stocks or bonds you can put up, or other assets), they may be obtained almost instantly.

Remember, if your goal is flipping you don't really care about the cost of the mortgage (since it's figured into the expenses of the deal). All you care about is keeping control of the property until you can dispose of it.

An asset-based bridge loan, or one that uses the property as collateral, may be just the answer.

Yes, institutional financing for investment property is not nearly as good as institutional financing for owner-occupied property. But, at least it's available. And that's a real step up compared to only a few years ago.

14
Unconventional Financing

In character, the actor Humphrey Bogart once said, "There's three ways of doing things: the right way, the Navy way, and my way!"

Something like this applies to real estate investment financing. In this chapter we're going to look at the last way, creative financing.

The traditional or "right way" of securing financing is to offer a down payment and then get an institutional loan. However, as we saw in the last chapter, this can be expensive and sometimes, depending on your income, next to impossible. So when things become impossible, it's time to do the improbable. And that's to get someone else to handle the financing for you. In most cases, that's the seller.

How Do I Handle Creative Flip Financing?

If you're planning to flip the property (see Chapter 3), you're only going to hold it for a short time. If you don't sell it out of escrow, you'll probably only be the owner for less than three months (assuming things go as planned). Therefore, why bother to get new financing at all? Why not simply keep the old financing in place?

I can hear old real estate agents rolling in their graves as I say this. The reason is that in today's markets, almost no mortgages allow for assumptions. (The exception are some adjustable rate loans, but they require qualifying as if you were getting a new loan.) When you buy a property, the terms of the existing mortgage normally call for it to be paid off in full. In other words, you can't leave the existing financing in place. At least, in theory.

129

In practice, things are different.

Let's consider what it is you want out of the financing. Basically, what you want is time. Time enough to find another buyer and get the property sold. That's probably going to take you no longer than three months. So, how do you buy yourself three months of time without getting a new mortgage?

Should I Dare Foreclosure?

One risk-taking investor I know dares foreclosure to accomplish this. He gambles that he can sell the property faster than the lender can foreclose. So far, he's been right every time. I don't advise this technique for the faint of heart! Here's how Jeff does it.

Jeff finds a property that he feels is flippable. He does an analysis and if everything checks out, he makes an offer to the seller in which he agrees to buy the property "subject to" the existing mortgage, not assuming it and not getting a new loan.

Buying "subject to" has some interesting consequences. It basically means that Jeff is not responsible for the repayment of the existing financing on the property. He agrees to make payments on the mortgage. But, if the mortgage goes into foreclosure, it's unlikely to appear on his credit. It will, however, appear on the credit of the original borrower.

Jeff is quite up front about this to the seller. He makes no bones about explaining what he plans to do. In a best case scenario, everyone wins. Some sellers simply won't go along, however, noting that foreclosure could adversely affect their credit. Others do, particularly those highly motivated to sell (see Chapter 5).

Jeff explains that the existing financing on the property undoubtedly contains an "alienation clause" which means that if title to the property is transferred to another party, the loan immediately becomes due and payable. In others words, the old mortgage can't be assumed (without the lender's permission, which normally isn't forthcoming).

So, Jeff explains, he's not going to assume it. He's going to leave it in place and simply try an end run. He'll buy the property subject to the existing loan remaining in place. Then, when Jeff resells within three months (hopefully), the rebuyer will get a new loan and pay off the old one, ending the problem.

The difficulty, however, is that if the lender finds out about the title transfer, it could go ahead and demand full payment on the loan, in effect, foreclose. (Many lenders really don't care and are perfectly happy to overlook such details for a mortgage that is performing well.) Jeff anticipates that even if the worst case scenario occurs, he'll be out of there with a rebuyer long before foreclosure can be completed.

TRAP

Judicial foreclosure (seldom used) can take as long as a year. Foreclosure on a trust deed (commonly used) takes a much shorter time, depending on the state involved. In California, the shortest time is about three and a half months.

Jeff, who's been doing this for some time, also knows that the odds are about 50/50 against the lender being told about the sale. In virtually all mortgages, when the loan is placed on the property, a reporting company contracts to notify the lender if and when title to that property has transferred.

However, in these days the servicing of mortgages changes hands very frequently. It is not uncommon for a borrower to learn that his lender of record has changed three times in a single year! As a result, the chances of the current loan servicer discovering a change of title is not all that good, as long as the payments keep rolling in.

Thus, Jeff figures that as long as he keeps making the payments over the short run, the lender will probably not bother to demand repayment of the mortgage. Of course, if the lender does, then it's a race between Jeff and the time clock to get rid of the property before foreclosure is completed.

TIP

Note, what we are talking about here is simply the triggering (or not triggering) of a mortgage clause with specific consequences spelled out. If a seller sells a house, the mortgage must be paid off. If you don't pay off the mortgage, you risk foreclosure. If you're willing to bear the consequences, there's nothing to say that you can't sell the house.

What About Using a Contract of Sale?

To further delay any chance of a lender placing the property into foreclosure, Jeff has taken to not even transferring title. Rather, he has the sellers give him a land contract of sale. This is an old form of transferring property used for years in bare land sales where the buyer couldn't come up with the full purchase price in cash. The seller gave the buyer a contract to buy which said that if and when the buyer ultimately came up with all the cash, title would be transferred—no cash, no title. The contract of sale, however, doesn't have to be recorded.

I don't have any idea how many properties are still transferred today using the contract of sale approach, but I wouldn't be surprised if it was in the 10 to 15 percent range. It's typically done for three reasons: The first, just noted, is to give the buyer time to come up with the cash while protecting the seller from giving title to a property not paid for.

The second is to avoid lawsuits. A buyer who is being threatened by lawsuits will sometimes acquire property using the land contract. Since the contract is not recorded, the buyer's name is not on the property and in a lawsuit that property is less likely to become involved.

Finally, a contract of sale is sometimes used to attempt circumvention of the alienation clause in modern mortgages. Again, since the contract is not recorded, the lender may not learn about the transfer and may not demand that the mortgage be paid.

TIP

Most modern mortgages include language which provides that any transfer, including a contract of sale, is enough to trigger the full repayment of the loan if the lender finds out.

The down side to using the contract of sale is that it is a most insecure position for a buyer. If the seller of a property decides that he wants to be dishonest, he can sell it again, even after he's first sold it to Jeff. Since recording of title is the means by which ownership is evidenced, and since Jeff doesn't record the contract of sale, this is possible. A savvy and dishonest seller could do Jeff in. Jeff says the risk is just another cost of doing business.

TIP

In many states a contract of sale can be recorded if at least one party that signs it has that signature notarized.

In flip financing, leaving the existing mortgage(s) in place may be your best alternative. It can be cheaper, more efficient, and a whole lot easier than trying to get a new institutional mortgage on the property.

TRAP

Don't take a chance with the lender for securing long-term financing—you could get burned. If you need long term, get it up front.

How Do I Come Up with the Down Payment?

Okay, you may be saying, that takes care of the financing. But what about the down payment? Chances are the existing mortgages on the property are quite low. How do I handle the difference, which could be 30 percent of the price or more?

The answer here is called creative financing.

Creative (or seller financing as it is more appropriately called) came into vogue in the 1950s. At that time the mortgage market was entirely different from what it is today. Virtually all residential mortgages were offered by savings and loan associations. And those organizations wanted to keep their loans in place. (They wanted to avoid the thousands it costs to replace a mortgage when a borrower pays off.) So they made all of those mortgages assumable. They wanted them assumed!

Indeed, there was almost always a penalty for paying them off early. Typically if you paid more than 20 percent of your mortgage in any year, there was a six month's interest penalty, a very heavy hit.

As a consequence, when people bought properties, they kept the existing loans rather than get new financing. However, that produced a problem of a different sort. As prices rose, the difference between the old loan and the new price increased, meaning that buyers had to come up with larger down payments. And, if there's one thing that buyers have trouble doing, it's coming up with a bigger down payment.

As a consequence, creative, or seller, financing came into vogue. The seller would give to the buyer a second mortgage equivalent to the difference between a 10 or 20 percent down payment and the existing assumable mortgage.

Perhaps an example will help here:

Example of Typical Seller Financing

Down payment	10,000
Seller financing loan	20,000 (new)
Existing mortgage	70,000 (assumable)
Sales price	**100,000**

In the above example, the seller has an existing assumable mortgage of $70,000 and a sales price of $100,000. That means the buyer must come up with the difference of $30,000.

However, there are very few buyers who can put 30 percent down. So, the seller "carries the paper" for $20,000 and the buyer only needs to come up with 10 percent ($10,000) down.

That's how it was done in the 50s and 60s.

But then in the 70s inflation came roaring out and lenders wanted to call in all those old low-interest existing assumable loans and replace them with high-paying, high-interest loans. So they did away with assumptions and we're where we are today.

But creative/seller financing still exists if you want to use it. It can replace most or even all of the down payment. It works the same way as in the old days.

Instead of giving the seller a cash down payment, you have the seller carry the financing. How much the seller will carry depends on what agreement you reach. You might put down 10 percent cash. Or 5 percent cash. Or even nothing! It all depends on what you both agree upon.

TIP

In the 1980s, creative financing got a bad name from unscrupulous buyers who bought with nothing down, using seller financing, and then never made a payment and ultimately let the properties go. The sellers were forced to foreclose to protect their investment and often ended up with little to nothing. Hence, today it's unlikely you'll find a seller foolish enough to accept creative financing and nothing down.

With flippable property it may be possible to have the seller carry back a second mortgage for most of the down payment, while you buy the home subject to an existing mortgage.

What About Long-Term Investing?

On the other hand, perhaps the property isn't flippable. Or perhaps you are worried that it might not be. Or maybe you just want to buy it long term. Are there any unconventional solutions available?

Indeed there are. Here, instead of trying to elude a lender's alienation clause, you look for a lender that allows assumption, or a seller that's got a property paid off (or nearly so). Here's how it works.

Many older FHA and VA mortgages are assumable (not all are—it depends on when they were issued). Look for a property with an older VA or FHA loan and you could find that the mortgage is assumable.

However, keep in mind that because it was issued long ago and has been somewhat paid down, and because since then prices have gone up, the existing assumable loan is likely to be for a smaller percentage of the property's value. Therefore, you'll need to have the seller give you financing (a second mortgage) as described above in order to avoid a big down payment.

The advantage here is that you can assume the existing mortgage and continue making payments without the threat of the lender demanding payment in full and going to foreclosure. It's a long-term solution.

TIP

Some of the older mortgages are assumable at the old interest rate. This could be good or bad, however, depending on what the rates were when the mortgage was issued.

Find a Paid-Off House

Another alternative is to find a paid-off property. If the sellers don't owe anything they may be willing to give you a new mortgage for close to the full amount of the purchase price. Even if they owe a small amount, they may be willing to pay this off with your down payment and give you a new mortgage themselves.

Why would sellers do this? If they are older and want to retire and the thought of regular income from a relatively high interest rate mortgage (when compared to low bank interest rates on savings accounts) can be quite appealing. Further, since it's a first mortgage, it's quite secure.

TIP

Make sure that any new mortgage that the sellers give to you is fully assumable. That way, you can use it to help the next buyer take over the property. If the sellers balk at full assumability, have it "one time" assumable. That way you can have it assumed by your rebuyer and you can get out of the deal.

With the increase in availability of institutional mortgages today (more appealing, as we saw in the last chapter, to investors) creative financing has almost been forgotten. But don't you forget about it. It can be an excellent way of buying investor property with little down. And if your intention is to flip, it can provide just the answers you need to gain control of the property and hold it for just long enough to get a rebuyer to take over.

Part 3

Renting in the Real World

15

Will It Make a Good Rental?

When buying for investment you have two choices, as we've noted earlier: You can flip the property. Or you can hold and rent until you can resell for a profit.

Assuming you can't (or don't want to) flip, your next question should be, will the property be a good rental? After all, if you can't rent it out, holding onto it can get to be very expensive!

Making the rental choice involves looking at four separate areas, which we'll consider in this chapter:

1. The location of the home
2. The type of home
3. The condition of the home
4. The economy

Is the Property in a Good Rental Area?

It's a truism that wherever there are people and homes, you can rent. However, some areas are better for rentals than others. Ideally you want your investment property to be in a good rental area.

TIP

You want to be able to get a high rental rate and be able to rent up quickly and keep the property rented. That's how to maximize your rental income.

What makes for a good rental area? It's simple—it's one in which there are many, highly salaried tenants available. Typically this is an area where there are a lot of high-paying jobs.

However, you want to be sure that your rental matches the types of jobs available. For example, if there's a manufacturing plant in town that provides a lot of stable blue-collar workers who can afford to pay up to $1,000 a month in rent, a property that you can rent for under $1,000 a month (and still pay your expenses) would be a sound investment.

On the other hand, a property where you needed to get $2,000 a month would make little sense in this area. You'd have nothing but long periods of vacancy.

On the other hand, perhaps in another community there's an industrial park that provides lots of high-paying white-collar workers who can easily afford to make $2,000 a month payments. Now, your home with the $2,000 rental makes good sense. On the other hand, you might actually have trouble renting out a home for only $1,000—it might be too small or lack features that the tenant population demanded.

In other words, your rental property must be suitable to the market in which it's located.

How Do I Determine the Local Market?

There are two ways to accomplish this: the hard way and the easy. The hard way is to spend some time investigating the area. Check with the local Chamber of Commerce for the types of employers in the area. Then call on the employers to find out what kind of tenants they are likely to offer.

Or, you can call a few real estate agents who specialize in property management and just ask. In a few sentences they should be able to tell you what the market's like. Further, if you have a particular house (or other property) in question, they should be able to give you a fairly accurate estimate of just how much you can rent it for. This is particularly the case if they are "farming" the area and know it very well.

Can you rely on such word-of-mouth opinions? I have. But to be sure, check the local newspaper rental section. This is usually divided up by area. Find the area your subject home is in and call a few landlords. Find out what they're offering and how much they're charging. You should be able to get a conclusive answer within three or four calls.

TIP

When you look at rental ads, also look for how many there are. A huge amount of ads suggests that perhaps there are too many rentals (or not enough renters) in your area.

How Do I Know If the House Will Make a Good Rental?

What you need to look for is a property without too many "angles." By angles I mean items that require TLC (Tender Loving Care). You want a property that will pretty much run itself because if there's one thing you can count on, it's that most tenants won't give the property TLC.

Avoid Older Property—Older homes need more care. Here's a list of problems that you, and your tenants, are likely to run into in older homes:

Problems of Older Homes

- **Plumbing distress**—from leaking faucets (which you have to run out and fix) to leaking pipes (which require moving the tenant out while the house is replumbed).

- **Electrical distress**—from light switches and plugs that suddenly burn out (which you have to run out and fix) to overloaded circuits which if not fixed can cause a fire. Older homes tend to have wiring that's too light-weight for today's modern appliances. Tenants can easily overload the circuits by plugging in too many heaters, lights, washers, or whatever in the same circuit, blowing fuses and circuit breakers. All of which can necessitate expensive rewiring.

- **Roof leaks**—You might put up with a bucket for awhile, but a tenant will want it fixed instantly.

- **Worn-out appliances**—You might keep them running for a few years by tenderly caring for them. Tenants will simply turn them on full and, if they don't work, expect instant replacements.

- **System problems**—from termites in the floor to bad heaters and bad air conditioning. If you're in the place, you can tolerate it awhile, or perhaps even do some of the repair or replacement work yourself. If it's a tenant, it will have to be done immediately, or you'll lose the tenant . . . and your rent.

A new house, preferably one less than 25 years old and ideally less than 10 years old, will largely avoid such problems. Newer properties have newer plumbing, electrical, roofs, appliances, and systems. There is far less chance of anything expensive going out.

Avoid Condos—Many people like the idea of buying a condo as a rental because the initial investment is usually lower than for a house. And while some people do successfully rent condos for years, overall I feel they make bad rentals.

The reason is the HOA (home owner's association). All condos are part of a HOA. And the HOA will set the rules for everything from changes you can make to the exterior, to noise in the evening, to where cars can be parked.

In other words, there are lots of rules. And while owners tend to follow these rules, if reluctantly, because they realize they are to keep up the overall value of the property, tenants have no such constraints. Tenants couldn't care less about property values, since they don't own the property. Hence, when renting a condo expect all sorts of continuing problems with the HOA. Expect your neighbor owners to complain at the drop of a hat about your tenant's activities. And expect to be fined and chastised by the HOA over what your tenants do. It's just so much hassle that it's usually not worth it.

Of course, as I say, some landlords do rent condos successfully. But then again, there are some people who are willing put their heads into a lion's mouth.

TIP

Doubly avoid trying to rent out co-ops. The control from the Board is far deeper and relentless than the HOA's control with a condo. Indeed, many Boards will have the right to veto any tenants you may want, unless they meet strict financial qualifications. (Sometimes, though not usually legitimate, the Board may require tenants to meet personal qualifications as well.)

Avoid Homes with Lots of Bedrooms—The problem is that the more people occupy the property, the more wear and tear (and potential damage) to it. This goes double for children, who in their play tend to bump, dent, gouge, and even chew up walls, floors, doors, and so forth.

The old adage from landlords years ago used to be, "I love children, in your place, not mine!" However, antidiscrimination laws prohibit you from refusing to rent to a family because it has children. You can, however, refuse to rent if the home is too small to accommodate the family. Therein lies the reason for not having too many bedrooms.

TIP

The fewer the bedrooms, the fewer the number of tenants and, as a result, the less wear and tear to the property.

While I've never found a hard and fast rule that says how many people at maximum can occupy a bedroom (some fire regulations put it at four!), it's a cinch that the more bedrooms you have, the more people can reasonably occupy the property. It stands to reason that a house with four bedrooms can have more people in it than a house with only one, even if both properties have the same square footage!

Does that mean that a one-bedroom house makes a good rental? Not usually. You won't find many tenants (or many buyers, subsequently) that only want one bedroom. But two- and three-bedroom properties do make good rentals, while four- and five-bedroom properties most certainly do not.

Avoid Big Lots—If you're the sort of person who likes room to roam, then buy a house with a big lot to live in. But, if you're an investor, avoid them like the plague.

A big lot requires big maintenance. If it has lots of lawn and land-scaping, you'll need to hire (and pay for) a gardener to take care of it. You can't count on the tenants to do that.

TIP

Look for automatic sprinklers in any rental. If the rental doesn't have a watering system, put it in. If the system isn't automatic, upgrade it. Don't count on a tenant to take care of watering for you. An automatic system will do the job.

The bigger the lot, the more upkeep involved. Yet, when it comes time to resell, you'll find that a big lot will only marginally return you any more money. In some markets, it may actually get a reduced price!

TRAP

Always pay the water bill yourself. (Have the tenants pay the other utilities). The only way you can be sure that your landscaping will be watered is if you're pay-ing for it. If the tenants pay the water bill, they may refuse to water the landscaping to cut costs. (After all, it's not their lawn, trees, and bushes that are dying.)

Avoid Pool Homes—There are two reasons: upkeep and liability. Until you have a pool, you can't believe how much upkeep is required to be sure it's clean and swimmable. Let a pool go and you'll find that algae very quickly destroys the plaster and filters, that equipment deteriorates, and that bringing it back up to par, if even possible, can be very costly.

A pool is also a big liability headache. There's always the chance that someone could fall in and drown. To protect yourself you'll need at least a five-foot fence with a self-closing gate all the way around the pool. And you'll need to rely on your tenants to maintain the fence and gate.

And even if the pool is protected, unless the water is properly fil-tered and cleaned, there's always the danger that a swimmer could get sick from swimming in it. You can be sure that if this happens and there's a lawsuit, you as owner/investor will be named.

TIP

It goes without saying that if you buy a rental with a pool, you'll want to carry a big liability insurance policy. The bigger the better, but I would never get less than $2 million. And this can also get expensive.

Always hire a pool service to maintain the pool. Don't rely on tenants to do this. Even if they want to, they often forget or do something incorrect that ends up costing you even more money.

Is It in Rental Condition?

A clean home will rent quickly to a clean tenant. But to sell a home, it will need to be more than just clean. It will have to look new.

If you fix up a property to rent, you only need go so far. Get it clean and you'll find a good tenant.

However, if you fix up a property to sell, you need to go much farther. You'll need to paint everywhere, recarpet, replace appliances, cabinets and countertops, and so forth.

Therefore, when buying a property that you plan to rent out, you don't need to look for a property that's been upgraded and is spotless. It only needs to be serviceable and clean. And this should be reflected in a more reasonable price.

On the other hand, if the property you're considering has been fixed up to sell, chances are the seller has spent a great deal of time, money, and effort on it. And this will be reflected in a higher price.

But as an investor looking to rent out a home, you don't really care about that extra effort made to bring the home up to selling condition. You're more interested in a lower price.

Therefore, don't pay for a Cadillac when you only need a Chevy. Don't buy a home for a rental that's been primped for sale. You're throwing your money away.

TRAP

Of course, you can always rent a thoroughly fixed-up home to tenants. However, chances are those tenants over the course of a few years will bring that home down to rental condition. By the time you're ready to resell years later, the home will still need a complete reconditioning.

What's the Economy Like?

When buying a property for investment, you'd be in error not to take into consideration the overall economy. You could do everything else right, and still be tripped up by a bad market.

There are really only two things you need consider from the perspective of the rental market and the overall economy. The first is whether times are good or bad. The second is the demand for housing in your area.

Put simply, when the economy is booming, lots of people have jobs and can afford to rent. In a booming economy, you'll do well buying a rental property.

TIP

Keep in mind that the economy is not homogenous. While overall it may be doing well, it could be doing badly in your area. Be sure you check the economy where you plan on buying your rental investment.

The second consideration is the supply and demand for housing. You want big demand, small supply. When it's the other way around, it's an indication not to buy an investment home.

Some areas of the country, such as the Northeast, have long had an oversupply of housing and a limited demand, though that has turned around in recent years. Other parts of the country, notably the South and in particular the northern part of California, have long had housing shortages and a high demand. (As of this writing, the demand for housing in California and some other parts of the country is far outstripping supply, pushing rental, and housing prices, to all time highs!)

The simple rule is to buy when and where the economy is good and the housing market is tight.

How do you know? Just read the local newspapers. You can count on frequent articles detailing information on this.

For a quicker answer, check with a local real estate board. They keep statistics on such things and can usually give you a quick answer. A local college with a real estate department is another good source.

When you buy an investment property that you need to rent out for a period of time, make your purchase wisely. Check out the location, the type of home, its condition, and the economy. Only when all say "go" should you make the leap.

16

Irwin's 12 Rules for Successful Landlording

I've been a landlord for over 30 years. I've rented residential property (from large apartment complexes down to single-family units) both for others as a broker and for myself. During that time I've had very few bad tenants. I would say that better than 97 percent of the tenants that I've had have paid all the rent that was due and left the property in acceptable shape.

My philosophy is that if I pick the right tenant in the beginning, things will work out in the end. A good tenant wants to pay the rent, on time, and wants to take care of the property. My job simply becomes allowing that tenant to do what comes naturally.

I'm sure that some readers who have had bad tenant experiences are shaking their heads. It may all sound like "pie in the sky" to them. Maybe. But, over the years I've developed some rules which have helped me out enormously. No, these 12 rules can't replace years of experience or even reading a thorough book on the subject. (Check out my book *The Landlord's Trouble Shooter*, Dearborn, 1999.) But these rules should give you a head start in some critical areas of landlording, and give you a taste of what's involved.

Rule #1—Remember, Business Is Business

Two things that we Americans celebrate are the notions of generosity and equality. I have seen first-time landlords bend over backward to

149

cater to the whims of their tenants. They accept late rents and provide unreasonable services all in the desire to prove that they are truly generous and want to treat their tenants as equals. Along the way they stop renting aggressively and usually end up paying for it financially.

The truth is that the landlord is in a much more financially demanding position than the tenant. As landlord you own the property. You stand to reap all the profits if values go up, and to lose a significant amount of money if they go down. You also have all the responsibilities of paying taxes, insurance, and mortgage interest, as well as paying for repairs. The tenant has none of those responsibilities. He or she only has to get the rent in on time and keep the place reasonably clean and tidy.

Because of the different responsibilities, you can never be on the same level as the tenant. The property is always going to mean more to you than the tenant. And you are always going to have to be in the position of having to hold tenants to the terms of tenancy they agreed to.

In short, renting property is not democracy in action. It's a business. You're more like a CEO and the tenant is more like an employee.

While this analogy is helpful, it's important not to stretch it too far. To counter tyrannical and unfair treatment by some landlords, the courts over the years have strengthened tenants' rights to the point where today many landlords feel that the tenants have the upper hand. In most states, the landlord is so restricted in what he or she can or can't do that some people say it just isn't worth renting out property any more.

I don't find that to be true. To my way of thinking, the courts and the legislatures have simply given tenants protections that they needed from unscrupulous landlords. If you're not unscrupulous, you should have little to worry about.

The whole point of this discussion is to note the importance of striking the right tone in your relationship with a tenant. You can't be arbitrary or dictatorial. Yet you can't be a wimp either.

You have to be in charge. It's your property and how you handle the tenant will largely determine what happens to it. Get your head straight. The tenant is not doing you a favor by renting from you—he or she needs shelter and has to rent from someone. On the other hand, you're not doing the tenant a favor—there are lots of other rentals.

Remember, it's a business and should be run as such. You're the boss and within the law, you set up the rules and see that they are followed. Keep to that thinking and you should do well.

TIP

Pick up a set of landlord/tenant laws appropriate to your state and study it before you begin renting. While the rules may differ from state to state, in almost all cases they are plainly stated, and you don't want to break them. A tenant lawsuit is no fun for anyone.

Rule #2—Offer a Clean Rental

The biblical observation "As you sow, so shall you reap" really does apply here. If the property you rent is clean when the tenant moves in, the chances are very good that it will be clean when the tenant moves out.

This should be obvious but it really isn't. I have known many landlords who really don't care what their property looks like. Their attitude seems to be, "I'm not going to live there, so what do I care? Let the tenants clean it if they want!"

That's not a very charitable attitude and it often comes from having a tenant who leaves the property a mess. However, having once been burned does not mean you need to fear fire. (It was Mark Twain who observed that a cat that jumps on a hot stove will never jump on a hot one again, or a cold one either, for that matter.)

Dirty and messy properties take far longer to rent, command lower rents, and attract a much lower-quality tenant. The person you really hurt when you fail to clean up your rental is you.

I always go through a rental and clean the carpets and floors, make sure the kitchen is spotless with the stove, refrigerator (if any), and the sink shiny and clean. I also repaint the walls as necessary. When prospective tenants walk in, I want them to think they are getting a place that's as good as new. That way, hopefully, they'll take pride in living there and take care of it.

TRAP

Sometimes when a property has a lot of tenants moving through it, it begins to take on a shabby appearance. After awhile the landlord tires of spending the money and time to clean it after each tenant and instead offers to pay for the paint and cleaning equipment if the tenant will do the clean-up work. This works only in a very limited way. If the property is already cleaned up, but a little bit on the worn side, and the tenant wants a gallon of paint to touch up a bedroom, by all means buy the paint. You probably have a very clean tenant who will take good care of the property. On the other hand, if the place is a mess and the tenant wants a gallon of paint to fix it up, don't buy the paint. Have the place fixed up before you go looking for a tenant. I've tried it both ways and I've found that tenants who are willing to rent a place that is a mess, even if they are willing to clean it up a bit, will still turn out to be poor quality tenants who have trouble making rent payments and who leave the place in even worse condition than they found it.

A good tenant simply won't accept a rental that's a mess. He or she won't want to spend much time cleaning (with the occasional exception of a fastidious tenant, as noted above). They know they are good tenants, they know they can find a clean place, and they will skip yours. As a result, you get what's left—the type of tenant you don't want.

TIP

If you do buy paint for the tenant or otherwise allow them to fix up the place, be sure that you choose the paint, wallpaper, or whatever. Always select the best possible quality (so it will last) and the most generic colors (so they will appeal to the most people). If you let the tenant make the selection you could end up with a purple bathroom and a red living room.

Rule #3—Take Care of the Water Bill

In most rentals the tenant pays the utility bills. This includes gas or oil, electricity, phone, and water. This is almost certainly the case with single-family residences where everything is separately metered.

There's nothing wrong with this unless you live in an arid climate and have a lot of landscaping. That landscaping will take water, and in arid climates water tends to be expensive. Don't expect any tenant to go out of his or her way to pay a big water bill to help your landscaping. Yes, most tenants do like nice landscaping. No, most tenants won't pay extra for it.

The answer is a water allowance. It doesn't have to be much. It doesn't even have to equal the costs the tenant will pay for all water actually used. It's just the idea that you're contributing. Each time the tenant thinks about not watering, he or she will remember that allowance, not get angry about the cost, and will water.

It doesn't work for every tenant, but it does work for many, and it could save you a lot of costs in relandscaping later on.

TIP

If you have large yards in front and back, you may want to consider providing a gardener. You can often charge more rent because you have a gardener, so there could be almost no cost to you, and it can mean keeping the property in great shape. If the property has a pool, a pool maintenance service is a must. Never rely on a tenant to take care of a pool.

Rule #4—Know Who You're Renting To

As suggested earlier, the way to get a tenant to take care of the property and pay the rent on time is to rent to the right tenant in the beginning. This is the biggest problem area for most new landlords—getting the right tenant. How do you do it?

Rest assured there is no guaranteed formula. There are, however, certain tips which will prove helpful.

Of course you will want to talk with the prospective tenants and form an opinion of them. (This is very important, and it is why I always suggest that you personally rent out the property.) Here are two critical areas to consider.

The Credit Report

Today, you as a landlord should have no trouble in getting a written credit report on a prospective tenant. All that you really need to do is to contact one of the local credit agencies (listed in your phone book), explain what you want, and have them send you some of their forms. The cost is usually under $25 for a brief report.

When you find likely tenant candidates, have them fill out the form, *being sure that they give you permission to check their credit history.* Then contact the credit reporting agency with your request. Usually within a day you'll have a printout of their credit history. Check it over carefully.

Ideally you're looking for tenants with no bad credit. They pay all their bills on time and have credit with a wide variety of lenders from credit card companies to department stores to banks. Chances are, however, you won't find this kind of tenant all the time (or even very often). More likely the person who rents has spotty credit, some good, some bad.

Study the credit report. If the prospective tenants have a lot of "late paying" notes, chances are your rent won't be paid on time, either. If they have some loan defaults or other failures to pay, you may not get your rent at all.

The credit report should be taken as an indication of how the prospective tenants view their credit. If they view it casually and don't really care, then you could end up with no rent. You want tenants who take their credit seriously and who regularly pay on time. One of the biggest mistakes is to "fall in love" with a tenant (not literally, but figuratively). The tenant seems ideal, until the credit report comes in. You look at the bad credit report, and then choose to ignore it because you're so convinced the tenant is wonderful. Bad move.

Ultimately it's a judgment call. Just remember, however, that if you decide not to give a bad credit report a lot of credence, then why did you order the credit report in the first place?

TIP

Give the tenant a chance to explain bad credit. Listen to the explanation. It may be perfectly logical, and the bad credit may not be the tenant's fault.

Previous Landlord's Recommendation

To me this is the single most important indicator of future tenant success. It's absolutely vital that you get the accurate name and phone number of the tenants' former landlords. It's a must that you get not just the previous landlord, but those going back two or three rentals. (If you just ask for the current landlord, you might get a wonderful recommendation from a landlord who's just dying to get rid of a tenant!)

Call up the former landlords and ask them about the tenant. Explain that you are planning to rent your property to this tenant. Ask for a recommendation.

Some landlords are pleased to tell you all they know. Others are hesitant to talk for fear that anything they say may later be used against them by the tenant. (Just as in employer/employee relationships, there have been cases where tenants have sued former landlords over bad recommendations.)

If the landlord is hesitant to volunteer information, you can ask questions that will get you the answers you want. For example:

"Would you rent to this tenant again? Why not?"

"Would you charge a higher cleaning/security deposit next time? Why?"

"Would you allow this tenant to have a pet?"

In nearly all cases you can quickly find out what you need to know from the former landlord. Listen carefully to what's said. Usually the former landlord has no axe to grind, unless the tenant moved out without paying rent, in which case the landlord may bend your ear telling you what a turkey the tenant was.

The credit report and former landlord recommendations are the two best sources of information about your prospective tenants. Don't skip either. They are important.

My Own Experiences

Having given you the rules about credit reports and former landlord's recommendations, let me say that I've broken them as well as kept them. I've rented to tenants with horrific credit reports. And I've rented to tenants whose former landlords told horror stories about them.

Why? A lot has to do with gut feelings and the tenants' explanations. In one case I rented to a tenant who explained that her bad credit was due to a boyfriend who left her with a lot of bills. It turned out to be the truth, and she was a great tenant. In another case I rented to a tenant whose former landlord said he left the place a mess with real damage done and never paid the rent on time. The tenant explained that he left it clean, paid the rent on time, but the former landlord was mad because he moved out over a dispute over painting. The former landlord had promised to repaint the insides of the house and reneged. I believed the story and he also turned out to be a great tenant.

As I said, it's a judgment call.

Rule #5—Don't Try to Avoid Children or Pets

This seems to fly in the face of advice that most landlords give. They say avoid renting to children whenever possible and avoid pets like the plague. Both can do damage to the property.

That certainly is true. However, the most reliable tenants tend to be the ones with kids. Family people tend to take care of property and pay the rent on time. If you try to avoid renting to families with kids, you may eliminate your best source of tenants.

Instead of not taking kids, try to rent to people who don't have more kids than the house can hold. A three bedroom, two bath house can easily accommodate two or three kids. It will, however, show wear and tear with six kids. Try to limit the number of children. (Also, be aware that small children sometimes write on the walls in crayon that won't come off and is very difficult to paint over.)

TRAP

You really don't have a choice. Depending on the circumstances, it is probably discrimination to deny a rental to a prospective tenant based solely on the fact that there are children in the family.

In the case of dogs, I follow the philosophy of an old friend who manages over 150 single-family residences. He says, "People always lie about dogs. They always say they don't have any and then, once they move in, the dog appears. So what's the point of saying no dogs in the rental agreement? Are you going to throw out a good tenant because he or she "acquires" a dog?

"Sometimes people come right out and say they have a dog. If I say no dogs, they say they'll get rid of the pet. I would never rent to anyone who would get rid of a pet.

"As a result, I simply say that one dog is okay. If there ends up being two, I look the other way. If there's a kennel, of course, I throw them out."

Cats and birds are something else. Cats which are not properly house trained may urinate on carpets. Cat urine is virtually impossible to get out. It may result in the need to get new padding under the carpeting, new carpets themselves, or even new flooring under the padding and the carpet! I always get a heftier cleaning deposit for a cat.

Birds can make a mess and they can leave a peculiar odor in the house which is hard, but not impossible, to remove. Also, birds can sometimes screech loudly at odd times during the day or night, disturbing others. I'd think twice about renting to a tenant with birds.

Rule #6—Don't Try to Get the Last Month's Rent

This must certainly fly in the face of advice that most people have received. The lease in which a landlord gets first and last month's rent has been the traditional rental agreement. To now suggest that a landlord not go for it might be tantamount to criticizing mom, baseball, and apple pie.

Yet, my advice is not to go for first and last month's rent. Here's why.

The traditional lease in which the tenant pays first and last month's rent grew mainly out of commercial usage. It's the sort of agreement you would use if you were renting a building to a commercial tenant. If the tenant didn't pay the rent on time, you could sue to collect the rent and you would always be one month ahead by collecting that last month's rent up front.

With a single house, however, realistically you're never going to sue to collect rent from a tenant who is in the premises and who isn't paying. You're simply going to want to get that tenant out and someone better in. Suing is the last thing you want to do. (You'll sue for unlawful detainer—eviction—when the tenant doesn't leave and doesn't pay—and you might hope to recoup the lost rent later as a result of that suit.)

There's another problem with first and last month's rent. What you are mainly interested in (besides collecting rent) is that the tenant leave the property in as good a shape as he or she found it. First and last month's rent doesn't address that issue—a security/cleaning deposit does. Yet, if you've already collected first and last month's rent, how large a security deposit can you realistically hope to get? For example, if the rent is a thousand dollars a month, first and last month's rent comes to $2,000. How much more can you expect a tenant to pay for a security deposit? $200? $500? You reach a point where your property requires too much cash up front for any likely tenant to afford it.

A better way is to forego the last month's rent paid in advance and instead get a very large cleaning/security deposit. Today most savvy landlord's are insisting on a security deposit at least equal to one month's rent if not more. If the property rents for $1,000 a month, before moving in the tenant would be required to come up with $1,000 first month's rent plus at least another $1,000 or $1,500 in a security deposit.

TRAP

Some states limit the size of a security/cleaning deposit. The maximum you can charge may only be one and a half to two times a month's rent.

The tenant who puts up that much money has something substantial to lose if the property isn't left clean. And if the tenant does not pay, the deposit can always be used to compensate for lost rent. A last month's rent cannot be used as a cleaning deposit. (Check with the laws in your state to be sure that security deposits can be combined with cleaning deposits and used for either reason.)

One concern is the savvy tenant who doesn't make the last month's rent payment. When you call about collecting the last month's rent, the tenant asks you to use the cleaning/security deposit!

You can write in the rental agreement that the cleaning/security deposit is NOT to be used as the last month's rent. You can argue until you're blue in the face. But the savvy tenant knows that it will take you more than a month to evict him or her and cost you a lot more than the security deposit, so that in the end, if they use it as the last month's rent there's not a whole lot you can do.

Usually most tenants are not that savvy (unless they've read this book!). However, even those that are and do tell you to use the cleaning/security deposit as the last month's rent will often leave the property respectably clean. The reason is that they don't want to get you too mad. If they leave the property dirty, you could always turn around and sue them in small claims court for the lost rent and the damage they did over the amount covered by the deposit.

TIP

Some states are now requiring landlords, even landlords of single-family residences, to keep security and cleaning deposits in a separate account and to pay the tenant interest on it. Check with a good property management firm in your state. Also, you may still use a "lease" without getting the last month's rent.

Rule #7—Rent for Less

It's important not to be penny-wise and pound foolish when you rent. The foolish landlord tries to get top dollar for a property. The wise landlord rents for just below the market.

The reasoning is simple—to get top dollar you have to wait for a tenant. If you rent just below the market, your property will always be full.

But, some newcomers to renting may ask, aren't you losing money that way?

Consider: You're renting a house where the market for a property such as yours is $1,000 a month. So you put your property up for

$970. You'll lose $30 a month because you're renting below market. At the end of a year it will mean a loss of $360.

On the other hand, you'll rent up immediately. All else being equal, tenants will choose your property first over similar properties renting at $1,000. Your property will be full all the time. (It's the same as when you go into the supermarket and see two products of equal quality next to each other—don't you buy the one that's five cents less than the other even though the price difference is negligible? Tenants act the same way.)

Now consider the landlord who insists on $1,000 a month. Assuming that the market value is correct, he will get it. But, it might take him a month until he finds a tenant. He will lose $1,000 of potential rent during that month. Is it better to lose $360 or $1,000?

But, some readers may say, you'll keep losing money year after year. After awhile the other landlord has a better deal because he's charging more.

Not at all. At the end of the year, if you have a strong tenant who wants to stay, raise your rent to the market level. If it's still $1,000, raise it to that point. The tenant shouldn't want to move because, after all, you've just adjusted the rent to the true market value. Besides, moving is a terrible hassle and no one wants to do it for a savings of $30 a month.

On the other hand, your competitor who started at the higher price can't raise rents because he or she would then be ABOVE the market.

What we're talking about here is the rent-up period. You want to get your property rented fast because every day it's vacant costs you money. Renting just below the market will accomplish this.

Rule #8—Charge for a Late Payment

This sometimes works for tenants who are always late. In any event it's a good idea to include it in every rental agreement you write.

The penalty typically takes this form: In the rental agreement you include a clause which says words to the effect that if that tenant does not get the rent in by a certain number of days after the due date (typically five days grace is given), there is a penalty. The penalty is usually $50 or 5 percent of the rent, whichever is smaller.

This rent penalty is no more enforceable than the overall rental contract (meaning that you have to go to court to get enforcement, which you would most likely not do over a $50 penalty charge). Nevertheless, in this modern world we are all conditioned to watch out for money penalties, and tenants are no different. You'd be surprised how careful they will be to get the rent in on time to avoid the penalty.

One caution—you have to enforce the clause. If the rent is late and does not contain the $50, you may want to refuse to accept the rent until the $50 is paid. This runs the small risk of not getting any rent. On the other hand, having once paid a penalty for late rent, the tenant probably will pay on time ever after.

A version of this works well with tenants who are already in the premises, who do not have such a clause in their lease, and who begin paying later and later each month. This is the rent discount. What you do is raise the rent for this tenant. Very carefully you explain that it's been so long since you've raised the rent, that your costs have gone up and so forth and, in conclusion, you feel that a $50 a month rent increase is warranted to take effect immediately (or upon termination of the current lease).

However, if the tenant gets the rent in on time, there will be a $50 discount. In other words, the rent may be $1,050. However, if the rent is delivered on time, it is reduced to $1,000. You'll be surprised how many tenants will work hard to get that rent in when due.

Rule #9—Don't Delay Fixing a Problem

When you become a landlord you also assume the duties of a "fix-it person." You are expected to take care of all the little as well as the big things that go wrong. This includes fixing leaky toilets, plugged drains, sprinkler systems that don't turn on, and light switches that don't work. What's more, you're expected to fix these things QUICKLY!

While you might put up with a leaky toilet for weeks, a tenant who feels he or she is paying big bucks for the property won't put up with them at all. When they want things fixed, they want them fixed yesterday. If you don't respond and at least make the attempt to promptly correct the situation, you could lose your tenant.

TRAP

Most states allow tenants to correct defective situations themselves and then deduct the cost from the rent. This is a definite "no-no" as far as you are concerned. The tenant might hire a plumber to fix a faucet and it would cost you $100, while you could have fixed it yourself for the cost of a 35 cent washer.

If you can't fix things yourself, get the services of a "handyman" who can. Rest assured there will always be something to fix and it's important to fix it, fast.

Rule #10—Keep a Lookout on Your Property

A rental property is a valuable asset. You may have hundreds of thousands of dollars invested in it. You've given it up to someone to live in for several hundreds of dollars month. But that doesn't mean they are going to look after that asset as you would. Therefore, check up on your property.

Don't wait until the tenant doesn't pay. Check up at least once a month, even it's only to just drive by.

Of course, you don't want to make a pest of yourself. Your rental agreement should give you the right to inspect the inside of the house with reasonable notice. But don't always be bothering a tenant who's paying the rent and keeping the place in good shape. As noted, just driving by once in awhile can be enough.

When you see those lawns start turning brown and the flowers in front drying up, you know you've got a problem. Stop by and check it out. It's better to find out early that your tenant lost his or her job. Maybe you can help your tenant find another job or at least another lower-cost rental.

Don't let things slip. You're the one who will get hurt in the long run.

Rule #11—Don't Let the Tenant Get Behind

What can you do when the payments are late and the penalty doesn't work?

This is another judgment call. Definitely speak to the tenant. Find out what the problem is. Maybe the tenant is waiting for a check to come in. If the late payment happens infrequently and there's a good reason, perhaps it's best to overlook it.

But what if the tenant is very late, one week, two week's late?

Remember, your cleaning/security deposit is typically only equal to one month's rent. If the tenant is two weeks late, he or she has already used up half the security deposit. Another two weeks and it's gone. Plus, if you have to evict, there's another month or two lost.

Most savvy landlords don't accept any late rent at all. If it's more than a day or two late, they call or check with the tenant to see what the problem is. With a good tenant, it's usually an oversight and after that the rent's right on time. With a bad tenant, you get excuses.

If the rent's more than a week late without sufficient explanation, savvy landlords send an official notice.

TIP

This can take various forms. Usually it's a three- or four-day notice telling the tenant to pay or quit (move out). The time length is determined by each state. It is normally the first step required in an eviction. You can pick it up at any stationery store or from an attorney's office. And tenants, particularly those who are regular late payers, know it.

One such notice is usually sufficient to convince a tenant that you mean business.

If the tenant still refuses to pay after two weeks, most savvy landlords begin eviction proceedings (discussed next). Note: waiting two weeks really doesn't cost you anything since most courts won't consider an unlawful detainer action until the tenant is at least two weeks late in rent and has used up the security/cleaning deposit.

The above time limits, however, are not set in stone. As with most things in renting property, it's a judgment call. On the one hand you don't want to scare, embarrass, or anger a good tenant into leaving just because one month they happened to overlook the rental due date. On the other hand, you don't want to give a bad tenant any more time than is absolutely necessary.

As I said, there is no one set answer. You have to play each case on it own merits. For myself, however, I would never let a tenant go more than two weeks without paying the rent no matter what the situation or how good I thought the tenant was. There's just too much at stake for me to lose.

Rule #12—Evict Only When Absolutely Necessary

Finally, you may at some time in your career as a landlord need to evict a tenant who won't pay the rent and who won't quit the premises.

TIP

Remember that do-it-yourself evictions where you physically throw the tenants out are no longer allowed in almost any area. Now you need the help of an eviction attorney.

Don't just call any attorney. Check around with local brokers, particularly those who handle property management. Usually there are one or two attorneys in town who do nothing but handle evictions. Call one. This attorney undoubtedly already has set fees and knows the ropes. This attorney can get the tenant out with a minimum amount of cost and time to you.

In addition be sure that the attorney gets a judgment against the tenant for back rent owed. Often the attorney, or his or her investigators can follow the former tenant to a new location and a new job and garnish wages to recoup your back rent. Usually their costs and fees are not deducted from the rent owed you. You may eventually get back everything you are owed! (Don't count on that happening every time, however.)

By the way, just getting the unlawful detainer judgment and eviction notice isn't the end. To finally get the bad tenant out, you will probably have to pay the sheriff. The officers will come and will literally move the tenant out. (Usually even the worst tenants will voluntarily leave once they realize that the sheriff is coming.)

TIP

When a nonpaying tenant won't quit, be prepared for a loss. Chances are you'll lose some rent, at least the rent until the tenant is evicted. You'll probably also get the place back in a mess, so there will be cleanup costs. Also note that some tenants cannot be evicted! In some states a tenant who is in the last stages of pregnancy or is seriously ill and can provide a doctor's letter that he or she cannot be moved, may be allowed to stay in the property—at your expense! A tenant involved in bankruptcy may make the eviction proceedings part of the bankruptcy, and postpone eviction. If you stay a landlord long enough, you'll see all kinds of problems.

The bottom line is that while all sorts of problems can happen, they rarely do. You may rent property all your life and never run into a quarter of the problems we've discussed in just this one chapter. On the other hand, you could be unlucky and get them all in the first year!

Most landlords are successful and go on to later sell their properties for hefty profits.

For more information on landlording, check into my book *The Landlord's Trouble Shooter*, Dearborn, 2nd Edition, 1999.

17

Turning an Alligator into a Cow

Although it may sound as though this is a chapter on animal husbandry, we're actually talking money here—positive money versus negative money (the kind that you must take out of your pocket each month just to keep your rental property going). And comparing real estate to animals just helps to get the point across.

A cow is a producing property. It gets milked every month, meaning that it delivers positive cash flow to you. It puts money into your pocket.

An alligator, on the other hand, is a property with lots of negative cash flow. It requires that you take money out of your pocket to feed it.

If you've ever had a cow or an alligator, you instantly know what I'm talking about. If this is new to you, then here's an example. You've bought a house that you consider a wonderful investment. However, after you're in, you discover to your dismay that the maximum you can rent it for is $1,000 a month. However your payments, including mortgage, taxes, insurance, maintenance, and repairs, are running $2,000 a month. That means that just to keep the property afloat, you have to put in a grand a month of your own money.

You can see why in the trade the property in the example above is called an "alligator." It is, financially speaking, eating you alive.

On the other hand, let's say you buy a property and discover that you actually have positive cash flow. With a "cow" applied to our previous example, you would be able to rent that property out for $2,200 a month—a $200 cash profit.

The cow provides you with milk and cream each month.

TIP

Notice that here we're talking strictly cash, not depreci-ation. Depreciation is a paper deduction that you take on investment real estate and which you may or may not be able to apply to your ordinary income for a tax sav-ings. (See Chapter 20 for a more detailed explanation.)

In Chapter 3 and elsewhere we've discussed how to buy a cow and how to avoid buying an alligator. But, sometimes the best laid plans go astray, and you could end up with just what you didn't want. What do you do then? That's what we'll answer in this chapter.

Exactly How Much Is Your Negative?

For some investors, each month brings a new surprise. They know they have negative cash flow, but they've never taken the time to fig-ure out exactly how much. They just know that at the beginning of the month when the payments are due, they always have to put in some cash from their regular account to cover their investment property account. I've heard investors say something like, "Gee, this month I thought it would be different."

Different? How? Why? It's easy to keep track of income—it's one check (or cash) paid to you. But, it's more difficult to track expens-es since there are both variable as well as regular costs. However, unless you have a handle on exactly what your expenses are, you can never turn an alligator into a cow.

Separate Accounts—The first rule of managing your real estate investment property is to set up a separate account for it. Don't com-mingle your rental monies with your personal monies. It's too hard to keep them straight, and it can be difficult later on to explain things if the Internal Revenue Service has questions.

TIP

If you have multiple properties, you don't need a sep-arate checking account for each, but you do need a separate bookkeeping account for each.

Your bookkeeping system can be quite simple. Do it in an accounts book or, even better, use one of the many accounting programs available for your computer. (Quicken has an excellent system.)

Set up your system so that you have two separate pages, one for income, the other for expenses.

Income—On the income side enter the address of the property and the name of the tenant. I also write down important facts such as when the lease is up (or if it's month-to-month), how large is the security deposit, the number of renters, and the number and type of pets. Then each month, write down when the rent check was received—the amount (just in case it's not a full payment) and the date. This way, later on, at a glance you can tell which tenants are paying regularly right on time, and which are frequently late and by how much.

Some rentals have income other than rent. For example, there can be income from rental washers and dryers, from soft drink machines, and so forth. You should have a separate heading beneath rental income for each other type of income you receive.

TIP

I always insist that rent be paid on the first of the month, so there's never an issue of the date due. When renting up property, sometimes the tenant will begin paying in the middle of the month. If that's the case, then I insist that the tenant pay one and a half month's rent the second month in order to catch up so payments are due on the first. The reason for having payments due on the first is because most people's rents are due on the first, so when tenants switch rentals they don't have to "break up" a payment. It is also usually easier to rent up a property on the first than on any other day of the month.

Setting up your ledger for income is usually quite simple.

Expense Accounts—Far more important in controlling expenses is to set up a ledger page for your expenses. This is more difficult because the amounts will typically vary from month to month. However, if you keep in mind that some expenses occur regularly while others only infrequently, it makes things easier.

Set up your page to first show all regular monthly payments. These typically include the following:

Typical Recurring Monthly Expenses on a Rental

- Mortgage payment (interest, principal, and taxes/insurance, if included in the bill)
- Water (and any other utility bill)
- Gardener, pool service, any other monthly service
- Home owner's fee

Next, add separate headings for infrequent expenses. Since you can usually determine what these will be, a defined heading for each is possible.

Typical Infrequent Monthly Expenses on a Rental

- Taxes (if paid annually or twice annually)
- Insurance (if paid annually)
- Maintenance—cost of work—plumber, electrician, handyman
- Repair—cost of materials
- Cleanup (when tenant moves out, to prepare for new tenant)
- Advertising (to find new tenant)
- Special—unanticipated expenses

TIP

It's important to set aside as a monthly expense any cost paid annually such as taxes or insurance. For example, if your taxes are $4,800 a year, set aside $400 a month. That way when the taxes are due, you'll have the money with which to pay them.

It should be obvious that the expense side of the journal needn't be extensive. It is, however, important that the last entry for unanticipated expenses be kept for items that occur just once. If an

expense pops up more than once, create a separate heading for it.
Here's how a typical journal will look:

Income/Expense Journal for Investment Property

Income		Date	Expense	
10-1-00	$1,500(rent)	10-1-00	$1,003	(Mort. pmnt.)
		10-1-00	300	(Tax prorate)
		10-1-00	47	(Ins. prorate)
		10-1-00	65	(Gardener)
		10-17-00	280	(Clean sewer)
		10-20-00	45	(Water)
		10-21-00	218	(Fix windows)
		10-27-00	517	(Replace Water heater)
			2,625	(TOTAL EXPENSES)

What should be clear is that this property is financially hemor-
rhaging. Just to keep the property afloat, the investor had to take a
total of $1,125 out of pocket this month.

However, a closer examination reveals that the property should
actually be able to achieve a positive cash flow. If you consider just
mortgage, taxes, and insurance, the total costs are only $1,350 a
month. With an income over $1,500 that's a positive situation, until
maintenance and repairs are added in.

The benefit of setting up a journal in this fashion is that it immediately shows what the problem is. The investor has to work at keeping down repairs and maintenance. If he or she is successful, the
income expenses will balance out over time. If not, the property will
eat the investor alive with expenses.

Can You Cut Expenses?

In our above example, it should be at least theoretically possible to
cut expenses because they are presumably only on an occasional
basis. The situation would actually be much worse if the monthly
negative remained the same, but instead of coming from repairs and
maintenance, it came from mortgage payment, taxes, and insurance.

These are the fixed expenses which are very difficult (but not impossible) to lower.

How, then, can you cut expenses? The answer is that you have to be creative. Let's consider each category:

Mortgage—A fixed expense, the only realistic way to cut this is to refinance to a lower interest rate or a different type of mortgage. A lower interest rate will produce a lower monthly payment. Moving from a fixed rate mortgage to an adjustable could also produce a lower monthly payment, at least for a few years. (This means that the investor will need to sell or refinance again after a few years when the adjustable's rate and monthly payments go up.)

Taxes—The only way to lower this amount is to have the property's tax value reassessed. But this is unlikely to produce a reduction unless property values overall have been dropping. (Indeed, a reassessment in a hot market can actually result in an increase in taxes!)

Insurance—It might be possible to produce a marginal reduction in costs by seeking out a cheaper insurance policy.

Water—The temptation is to make the tenants pay for water (as they do for other utilities) and cut this cost. That, however, would be a mistake. The result could be the tenants cutting back on watering the landscaping, which would then die and would adversely affect the overall value of the property.

Gardener—Again, a mistake to cut because the gardener will maintain the landscaping. An alternative is for the investor/owner to spend a few days a month doing the gardening.

Maintenance—This has been a heavy expense. If you call a plumber out to fix a washer, you may incur $100 charge for a 25-cent part. Most investors cut these costs to the bare minimum by doing the work themselves.

Repair—It could be argued that this investor was just unlucky. There was a water heater replacement. Perhaps there won't be any more repairs for the rest of the year . . . or not. If it's an older property, repairs will be a constant problem. The solution is to buy more wisely by purchasing a newer home with fewer such problems. Once purchased however, the only alternative is to seek the cheapest repair possible. Sometimes this involves the owner/investor doing the work himself or herself. Other times it means getting three or four bids until you get the least expensive.

Special—Good news here for the investor in our example—no special unanticipated expenses cropping up.

TRAP

As noted in the last chapter, you can't put off maintenance and repairs in a rental the way you might be able to in your own house. You might tolerate no hot water or a leaky roof for a few days or longer. Tenants won't. They feel they are paying rent (sometimes a very high rent) and their expectations are that the premises will be habitable and at least in as good a condition as when they originally rented. It's up to you to make it so.

Can I Raise Rents?

I used to have an investor friend whose standard advice was, "Don't turn off the lights, increase income." He was saying that the way to make money was not to worry about expenses, at least not those that were unavoidable. The way to profit was to increase income. In our above example, even with the heavy repair and maintenance expenses, it would all come out okay if income could be increased to say $2,200 or $2,300 a month.

Can you increase rents to cover your expenses?

Regardless of what my friend thought, it's unlikely. You *can* do some things to make the property more valuable to renters.

You can make it spotless, add a gardener or a pool service, or add some furniture as needed.

Doing all the above might get you a hundred dollars over market, perhaps even $200, but at the same time it will cost you money to do those things.

Overall, rentals go pretty much for their market value. And that's mostly determined by their competition, location, and size. And you can't give your rental a new location, or easily make it bigger.

TIP

Sometimes you can convert inside areas to your advantage. For example, a study or den might be converted to a bedroom. Going from a two-bedroom rental to a three-bedroom could increase rent by 20 percent or more.

All of which is to say that barring a big change in the rental market upward, you're pretty much going be stuck with rental income. Of course, be sure that you're charging as much as the unit warrants—don't charge less. But, don't hold out hopes of charging more.

TRAP

As noted earlier, it's a mistake to charge even $50 over market. The difference could be between renting up immediately or waiting a month or two for a tenant who will pay more. Yes, your monthly income will be higher. But, it could take years to make up for rent lost in the month or two it took to find that higher-paying tenant.

Can Tax Savings Help?

Some investors feel that they can easily afford to sustain a cash loss on their rental property because they'll make it up in tax savings at the end of the year. This may or may not be a reasonable assumption.

We'll go into taxes on investment rentals in Chapter 20 in more detail. But suffice to say that unless your personal income is under $100,000 a year, you won't be able to deduct all your losses on your rental property (either cash or from depreciation) each year. If your personal income is over $150,000, you may not be able to immediately deduct any losses from rental income!

Further, there's a big misconception among those who are completely unfamiliar with tax deductions as to how they work. (Those of you who regularly handle rental income deductions can move on.)

If allowed, you can take the loss on your rental property as a *deduction* against your other ordinary income. You cannot take it as a *credit*. What's the difference? A deduction lowers the income on which you pay taxes. For example, if your taxable income is $50,000 and you have a rental loss of $10,000, your taxable income is reduced to $40,000.

A credit, on the other hand, is a reduction of your taxes. If you owe $12,000 in taxes and you have a $10,000 tax credit, your taxes are reduced to $2,000.

Losses on rental property, when allowed, are a deduction, not a credit. They reduce your income and, depending on your tax bracket, result in some tax savings. They do not directly reduce the taxes you owe.

Get Professional Advice

Even if you never have before, when you first buy rental property you should get a good accountant to look over your tax situation. Your accountant should be able to tell you quite accurately what tax savings, if any, you'll get from owning the property. If you have savings, then you can apply these against your monthly negative to reduce it.

TRAP

Keep in mind that what the government giveth, it also taketh away. Tax savings received each month based on depreciation usually act to lower your tax basis. This means that when it comes time to sell, you could owe more in capital gains. However, the capital gains tax rate is relatively low (compared to what it was in previous years), which means that you may find this still an advantage.

The best way to get rid of an alligator is to never buy it in the first place. Buy a cow and you'll get plenty of milk from your property. Buy an alligator and you'll spend all your time trying to devise ways to keep it from eating you alive.

Part 4

Selling for Profit

18

Selling a Rental, Fast

It's been three years since you bought the property, when prices were much lower. Since then they've taken a spurt upward. Now, they've plateaued. You sense you're at a peak and you want to get your profit out. But to do so you must sell, fast. How do you do it?

How Do I Get the Tenant Out?

The first step, of course, is to remove the tenant. While you can sell a property with a tenant in it, it's much harder, particularly if you want to sell to the wider market of owner-occupants.

Needing to get the tenant out on short notice is the best argument I can think of for using a month-to-month rental agreement. Under the terms of such a tenancy, either you or the tenant can terminate the arrangement simply by giving 30 days written notice. Just tell the tenant to leave in a month. What could be easier?

TIP

Sometimes tenants will find it hard to pick up and move on such short notice, particularly those who have been there a long time. Nevertheless, if you're insistent they will usually go. After all, there are always plenty of other rentals. A tenant who refuses, however,

179

is subject to removal and, barring extenuating circumstances noted below, you are likely to get a swift eviction.

Many investor/landlords prefer a long-term lease. With a lease, the sale is subject to the tenancy. If the lease has eight months left to run and you want to sell right now, the tenant has the right to remain in the property for eight more months. This is a big reason not to use a lease.

TRAP

Contrary to common belief, a lease does not benefit the landlord. Instead, it ties the landlord's hands in at least two ways: the inability to remove the tenant and the inability to raise rents. On the other hand, the presumed benefit of the lease, tying a tenant to the property, is largely illusory. If the tenant leaves during the lease term, you as landlord are required to mitigate any damages by renting again as soon as possible. Further, you can only sue to get your lost rent as the rent comes due each month. Finally, in many cases it's hard to track down a tenant who packs up in the night and disappears. A residential lease is not all that it's cracked up to be.

If you had the foresight to set up a month-to-month tenancy, removing the tenant should be fairly easy. On the other hand, if you signed a lease, you may have to use more creative means to remove the tenant.

How Do I Break the Lease?

Depending on how the lease was written, you may or may not have various outs. If the tenant was late with rent, or has not kept the property in good shape, or has done something else to violate the terms of the lease, you could have a lease breaker.

Simply confront the tenant with the facts and point out the alternatives—either the tenant leaves in a reasonable amount of time (30 days), or you'll take the tenant to court over the lease breaker. Most residential tenants will prefer to leave than to fight with an angry landlord.

TIP

If the tenant does fight, however, you will have to prove that there is, in fact, a lease breaker and that you did give the tenant an opportunity to make good and the tenant refused. That's not always such an easy row to hoe.

If there is no lease breaker, or the tenant is adamant about staying, then you may want to try to make a financial settlement. If, for example, there are eight months left on the lease, you may want to pay the tenant four months rent to move out immediately.

What! You may be asking yourself if you read that correctly—pay the tenant?!

Yes, pay the tenant to get back your right to occupy the property. The tenant has the right for eight months, so it will cost you something to get that right back. Of course, don't start by offering four months— start by offering a month's rent back and increase as necessary.

By the time you get to half the remaining lease period, almost all tenants will be eager to move. After all, they can take your money and go elsewhere and live rent free for a few months. That's an offer that's hard to pass up.

What If the Tenant Simply Refuses to Leave?

I've never had a tenant who refused to leave after being given a money inducement. However, I have heard of it happening. If that's the case, then if it's a lease, you'll simply have to wait the tenant out or try to sell the property with the tenant still inside, a tough proposition.

Of course, if you've got a month-to-month arrangement and the tenant refuses to go after proper notice, simply begin an unlawful detainer action. Find a good local attorney who handles evictions and let him or her go at it. The cost is usually around $1,500.

TIP

You could have a serious problem if the tenant is in the later stages of pregnancy or is seriously ill. A judge might hesitate to force such a tenant out just so you could sell your property at a profit.

Should I Fix Up the Property?

If you don't fix up the property, you'll get a lower price and a delayed sale. Remember, there's tenant-ready and buyer-ready and the two are completely different. Even if the tenant leaves the property in the exact same condition as it was when it was first rented, chances are it's going to be far from buyer-ready.

Here are some of the things you'll need to consider when fixing up a rental:

TIP

A lot will depend on the condition of the property. Some properties will take a lot of work, others much less.

Fix-Up Work to Get a Rental Ready for Sale

- **Upgrade landscaping**—For the tenant perhaps a lawn and few shrubs were satisfactory. For sale, however, you'll want to dress up the look of the land. That means adding flowering plants, cultivating gardens, and making sure the existing lawn and shrubs are full, green, and trimmed. All this is not usually expensive, but it can take time to accomplish.

- **Cleaning driveway and front walkway**—This is what the potential buyer will first see. You'll want to get out any oil and rust stains. For an asphalt driveway that means recoating to give it a new look. For a concrete driveway with cracks I suggest cutting out the cracks and cementing again, or adding brickwork. Yes, this latter can be expensive but it's usually worth the cost in terms of a quicker sale for more money. Remember the quality of the front of the home sets up the buyer's anticipation of the home's quality overall.

- **Painting**—It goes without saying that everything inside and out that is the least bit dingy, dirty, peeling, or otherwise less than perfect should be painted. Use good paint and be sure it's a professional quality job. This is where it shows.

- **Carpeting**—At the least have it cleaned. If it's worn or has stains that won't come out, replace it. These days you can get inexpensive carpeting that looks good (at least for awhile). This will help the house immensely.

- **Resurfacing cabinets and counters**—Kitchens and baths sell the home. If the house is over 10 years old, consider a minor remodel of these areas. Repainting or resurfacing cabinets is not that costly and makes a huge difference. Installing new countertops of tile, Formica, stone, or Corian brings the home up to a new level of elegance (and price). Yes, this is where it gets expensive.

- **Fix-Up**—Do what it takes to get any area of the house that looks bad into good shape. Remember, the house is only as good as its weakest link. A bad bedroom or a dilapidated basement or garage can ruin the image of quality that you want to portray.

How Much Should I Spend/How Much Should I Upgrade?

When you sell you want top dollar for your home. However, you don't want to overdo it. Spend too much fixing and cleaning and you won't get your money out.

Let your guide be the neighborhood norms. Check out other homes for sale in the neighborhood. See what they look like and then compare them to yours. If they all have expensive granite countertops and yours has inexpensive old Formica, upgrade to granite. You'll get your money back and more.

On the other hand, if all the homes have less expensive tile, then don't go for more expensive Corian. Just clean the tile you already have, or if it's in bad shape replace it with the same material.

For much more information on what to do and how much to spend, check into my book *Tips & Traps When Renovating Your Home*, McGraw-Hill, 1999.

Can I Get a Second Opinion?

Yes, and it's a good idea to do so. Just because you're a buyer of real estate, doesn't mean you're great at selling it. Get a pro to come in and take a look at the property. I'm speaking here of a good agent or two.

Agents deal with homes day in and day out. They see properties in good shape, bad shape, and every flavor in between. They can walk through a home in five minutes and tell you what all of the bad features are and what you should do to correct them.

The opinion of a good agent is invaluable . . . and easily obtained. Just say that you are thinking of selling your house, will consider the agent for a listing, but for now just want to know how well it shows. Agents will line up for the chance to tell you. (We'll have more to say about finding a good agent shortly.)

Listen to what the agent says. Think about it. It may seem a totally foreign idea to you. But chances are it's correct.

How Do I Estimate What It Will Cost to Fix Up the Property?

Simple—ask the experts.

After you've determined what needs to be done (see above), call in the pros who regularly do it. If you need carpeting, call in a carpet supplier.

TIP

If you haven't already discovered this, there are carpet wholesalers that cater to owners of investment real estate and who offer greatly reduced prices. Check with an agent who handles property management to find one of these in your area.

If you're going to have countertops put in, call people who do this kind of work. The same holds true for installing sinks and appliances, hardwood floors, and wall paneling.

But, also consider doing it yourself or hiring a handyperson to do it. While some work that involves the structure of the property or electricity, gas, or plumbing will demand a pro, much other work can be done by almost anyone.

You can save a huge amount of money by doing work yourself or hiring a helper. Just keep in mind, however, that the proof is in the pudding. You need to get a good result, a job that looks good, and will help sell the property. If you or someone you hire hourly does the work and it turns out badly, it will have the opposite effect. It will just make the property harder to sell.

Should I List with an Agent or Sell It Myself?

The statistics suggest that about 85 percent of all residential property is agent sold; and only 15 percent is handled by owners. There's a reason.

Agents have the system. They have the MLS (Multiple Listing Service), they have the buyers (who normally seek them out first), they have the experience, and it's what they do for a living. Quite frankly, to get a quick sale, you're best off listing your property with an agent.

Of course, agents also charge a hefty commission. If your property is in the $300,000 range and the agent charges 6 percent, that's $18,000 off the top that you'll need to spend. To save all or a part of the commission, you might want to consider at least trying to sell on your own.

How Do I Find a Good Agent?

To find a good agent, you have to know what makes one good. The answer to this is that you want an agent with all of the following characteristics:

- **Honest**—The last thing you want is to be told one thing and discover later that it's something else.

- **Experienced**—You don't want to be the client that the agent learns on. You want someone with years of experience.

- **Local**—You want an agent who knows the market where your property is, like the back of their hand. You shouldn't be telling them price and comparables, they should be telling you without even having to look them up.

- **Connected**—You want your agent to take advantage of the system that's in place. That means getting the message across to the hundreds of other agents that your property is a good deal. This can include talking your property up at agent meetings, caravaning agents to your house, and holding agent-only open houses.
- **Amiable**—In addition to being a financial advisor, a good agent will also be your friend.
- **Assertive**—The agent must be strong enough to get your price from a buyer.

Do such agents exist? Yes, they certainly do. But, you have to do some interviewing to find them. Don't expect the first agent to cross under your transom to be perfect. Look for referrals from friends and associates. Ask the agent for recommendations from satisfied clients (at least three). Check with the Better Business Bureau and even the local district attorney for any complaints. Do the same due-diligence you would if you were entrusting a couple of hundred thousand dollars to a finance person. You are!

How Do I Sell It Myself?

I always advise every seller to give selling "by owner" a shot. You won't know if you could have done it unless you try. But set a time limit, say a month or two. If you haven't successfully sold it by then, bite the bullet and go with a professional.

If you're going to sell by yourself, don't give up on the idea of using agents. You can usually give a buyer's agent half a commission to handle the sale for you and bring in a buyer. Half a loaf is better than none at all. Just put "Will Co-broke" on your sign. Agents will know what you mean.

Besides co-broking, however, you'll have to do all of the other work yourself. If you're going to sell by owner, you'll need to do all of the following:

The Work of Selling Your Own Home*

1. Fix up the property (which you'll have to do in any event).

---

* The list is from my recent book, *Robert Irwin's PowerTips or Selling Your Home For More*, McGraw-Hill, 2000.

2. Get a sign and stick it in the front yard.

3. Arrange and pay for newspaper advertising.

4. List your home on free services on the Internet.

5. Hold your own "Open House," allowing anyone who shows up to go through your home.

6. Go to local companies and solicit the help of their transfer departments.

7. Create an advertisement to go on a public access channel of a local TV station.

8. Create flyers and put them out on your "For Sale" sign, in grocery stores, and on other bulletin boards.

9. Be home at all times to catch phone calls from potential buyers. Yes, you can use an answering machine, but buyers often won't leave their name and number . . . you need to talk to them directly.

10. "Sell" your home over the phone when buyers call.

11. Show your home to those buyers who call. Remember, nobody but you is screening these people. And there are some criminals out there who do make it a point of checking out FSBOs for future robberies and worse.

12. When you find a buyer, negotiate directly over price and terms.

13. Handle the paper work which includes
    - A sales agreement,
    - Disclosures,
    - Settlement documents,
    - Inspection reports, and
    - Escrow opening and closing instructions.

14. Obtain a termite clearance. (The buyer won't be able to obtain financing without it.) Arrange for any termite repair work.

15. Clear the title to your property in case there are any liens or encumbrances that need to be removed.

16. Manage the escrow.

17. Deal with the buyer's anxieties and problems during the closing period.

18. Let the buyer have a "final walk-through."

19. Handle a buyer who wants/needs to pull out of the deal after the agreement is signed.

20. Move(which you have to do anyway).

This list is not designed to intimidate you, but rather to realistically show what's involved. If you don't want to do the work, don't try selling the property on your own. Agents really do earn the commissions they charge!

Once I Find a Buyer, How Do I Handle Disclosures and Inspections?

Whether you sell through an agent or by yourself, you'll need to give the buyer disclosures on your property. And you'll need to allow the buyer the opportunity to have a professional inspection.

TIP

It's to your advantage to offer disclosures and insist on a buyer's inspection. This way, the buyers can't later come back and claim that some defect was hidden which would have led them to offer less or to not even buy the property. You don't want those kinds of problems.

The problem with investment real estate is that because you weren't living in the property, you may not know of all of its problems.

It's easy to assume that because you've been fixing everything that the tenant called about, you know everything that is wrong with your rental house. But, the tenant may not have called about everything. For example, the roof may regularly leak. But because it only produced a few stains on upstairs room ceilings and no actual water dripping, the tenant never bothered to call. You just assume the roof is okay.

Or there may be serious cracks in the slab or foundation. But because the tenant never noticed anything through the wall-to-wall carpeting and never said anything, you weren't aware of it either.

If you're actually living in a home day in and day out, you'll notice far more than if you just visit it once every month or so for a few minutes.

Therefore, it's to your advantage to conduct your own thorough inspection of the property after the tenant moves out and prior to sale. You don't need to hire a professional inspector (although you may want to); you can do it yourself. Spend a day or so in the property. Check for water marks on ceilings, in the attic, and in basements. Walk all around the perimeter looking at the foundation, the siding, the paint, the roof line, the gutters, and so on. Wiggle the fence to see if it's weak. Walk the yard to check for small sinkholes. In short, spend some time learning about your property.

TIP

Whenever I sell a rental house, I always spend at least one night in it. It doesn't take much effort to haul in a comfortable air mattress. It's positively amazing what you can learn from dripping faucets to barking dogs, to creaking and groaning beams.

See No Evil, Hear No Evil, Speak No Evil

The other alternative, advocated by some, is to disclose to the buyers only what you actually know without investigation, which is probably nothing. As a result, your disclosures are clean. How can a buyer refuse?

Yes, but what if there's something seriously wrong with a house that the buyer later says you should have known about?

My own feeling is that it's better to get any problems out in the open during the negotiating period after the buyer makes an acceptable offer and before the deal closes. Once the deal is closed I don't want to lie awake at night worrying that someone might be calling to tell me they've discovered a problem and telling me that I certainly should have known about the problem.

Closing the Deal

Closing the sale of a rental home should not be much different from any other closing. It's mostly up to the buyer to come through with the financing. Once that's done, and any contingencies are removed, all you have to do is provide clear title.

The only catch is that you also must provide a ready-to-go home. Presumably the tenant is out or you've reach agreement with the buyer on the tenant staying.

The home has been cleaned. The final walk-through by the buyer goes smoothly, and you're out!

19
Converting a Tenant to a Buyer

If your goal is to eventually sell for a profit (and it may not be, as we saw in Chapter 2), then you want to lock in a buyer as soon as possible. Ideally, you'd like to arrange for a rebuyer when you make your own purchase.

Of course, if you're planning to hold and rent for several years, this may seem like an impossible dream. Yet, it really isn't. As we saw back in Chapter 2, by using a lease-option you can arrange for the sale of your investment property years downstream, and do it almost as soon as you purchase it.

The idea here is to have the person to whom you're going to rent the property be the same person who will eventually buy the property. Convert your tenant and you have the perfect buyer.

Is There a Perfect Buyer?

Who could be a better buyer for your property than the tenant who is already living in it? Think of the advantages:

- The tenant already knows the property—you don't have to show it to him or her
- The tenant has plenty of time to acquire the needed down payment as well as to arrange for financing
- As a future owner, the tenant will take extra care of the property

Of course, not all tenants are suitable buyers. Some don't have the cash. Others don't have the income to qualify for an appropriate mortgage. And a great many others are simply happy to rent—they don't want to buy.

All of which is to say that while a tenant can be a perfect buyer, not all tenants are. The question is how to find just the right tenant.

How Do I Find the Tenant-Buyer?

One method is to simply rent the property to the best available tenant. Then, a few years later when you're ready to sell, you simply ask the tenant, "Would you like to buy the home in which you're living?"

Chances are, however, you'll get a negative answer. Most tenants, I have found, would rather move to another place—another rental or even a different owned home—than buy the property in which they are living. Converting a tenant to a buyer *at the end of the rental period* can be a hard sell.

On the other hand, if you sell the tenant on the idea of eventually purchasing the property at the time you first rent to them, it's a different matter entirely. Then, during their entire rental stay they will be seeing the property in a different light. It will be their permanent home. They are simply renting it until it's convenient to make the purchase.

In short, instead of looking for a tenant when you want to rent up your investment property, look for a buyer who will be willing to handle a delayed purchase.

What Is a Delayed Purchase?

Today more people than ever before in history own their own homes in the United States. And many more would love to do so. People in general understand that an owned home is a great investment: it provides financial security, privacy, and most of all, profit.

However, a great many people simply can't afford to buy outright. Rather, while their first desire is to purchase, their wallet dictates waiting.

This is the person you want as a tenant—the not-quite-ready-to-buy, buyer.

How do you find this person? You advertise!

Where Will I Find a Delayed Buyer?

Even if you're not familiar with this approach, you've probably seen the ads for delayed buyers in local newspapers. They usually read something like "Rent To Own!" or "Rent Now, Buy Later!" They sometimes will appear in the rental section, rather than in the homes for sale section, although placing them in either location works.

The idea here is that you're looking for more than a tenant. You don't want someone with a strictly rental mind-set. You want someone who is thinking ahead to ownership. When you qualify this person you actually do two different kinds of checking up. In the first case, you look at them as potential tenants, with all of the checks mentioned in Chapter 16. In the second case, you also qualify them as a purchaser.

This means that you determine whether or not they can qualify for a mortgage big enough to handle your property, and whether or not they can come up with enough cash for the down payment within the next two or three years (or however long you plan to rent before selling). A few quick calls to a loan broker (made with their cooperation) will usually answer the first question. The second, however, usually requires a bit of guesswork on your part.

TIP

As we've seen, financing these days has changed to the point where it is possible for buyers to get into a property with as little as 3 percent down (and in some cases, nothing at all down). This means, however, that they must be very low credit risks and, unfortunately, oftentimes tenants do not fill this ticket. Therefore, you must determine how big a down payment they will realistically need to buy your property and what the actual chances are that they can come up with the money.

Should I Use the Lease-Option?

As noted, in Chapter 2 we discussed the basics of a lease-option. Now, we're going to look at it in more detail.

A Lease—You enter into a tenancy agreement with the tenant. This is in the form of a standard lease. It is for a specific period of time and a total amount of rent. The time can be for a year, three years, or whatever. The form usually specifies what the tenant may and may not do to the property, includes a security/cleaning deposit, addresses the issue of pets, the number of occupants, and so on. It's exactly the same sort of rental agreement that you would use if you were simply involved in being a landlord.

TIP

The lease does not need to include the last month's rent, although it may if you and the tenant agree on it. Sometimes it's an advantage not to include the last month's rent, but instead to have a larger security/cleaning deposit. The reason is that the last month's rent cannot be applied to cleaning and some security issues, while a cleaning/security deposit can be applied to missed rental payments—see Chapter 16.

An Option—You also give the tenant an option to purchase the property. In its concept, this is no different from any other option whether it involves stocks or real estate. It gives the tenants the choice of buying the property at some future date.

TIP

Note that the option favors the tenants—it's their right to buy. You are locked into selling IF they choose to execute their option. Of course, since you want to sell, this is exactly what you're hoping they will do!

The Combo—The lease and the option are usually locked together in several ways. For one, you presumably would not offer the option unless the other party also agreed to rent your property. And you would not allow them to rent your house unless they also agreed to take the option to purchase.

Further, it is common for optionees (the tenants) to pay for the privilege. They might, for example, give you $1,000 (in addition to any rent monies) exclusively for the right to get the option. Any option money you get is yours. It never has to be returned, although it is usually considered part of the purchase price when the tenants eventually buy. Separate option money, however, is not normally required for the option to be valid. You can consider the first month's rent, for example, as the option money.

TIP

My own experience is that you'll do better if the tenants put up some separate option money and understand that it will go toward the purchase price, when they buy. It doesn't have to be much, even just $500 will do. What it does is it cements the idea of the purchase in the minds of the tenants. By putting up that nonrefundable amount they become locked into the concept of purchasing the home and putting that money to good use. They always remember that if they don't purchase, the money is lost.

Rent Applied to Purchase

The real key to the lease-option, however, is that you will give a portion of each month's rent toward the down payment required to make the purchase of the property. Mention this and you will see potential tenants' ears perk right up. They will instantly see the benefit to themselves.

That's correct. You will apply a portion of each month's rent toward the eventual down payment. Be sure you understand this important angle: if the rent is $1,000, you might apply $400 toward the down payment. This means that at the end of a year, the tenants would have $4,800 in credit toward a down payment. The amount would swell to almost $15,000 by the end of the three years.

Tenants who are cash poor immediately see this as an easy way to get into ownership. If saving was hard for them, this is as simple as falling off a log. If you're honest, something they will want to be assured of, they know that their nest egg is growing with each monthly payment. This is a far cry from paying normal rent, where the money is simply lost.

TIP

The success or failure of the lease-option (as measured by whether or not the tenants eventually convert to buyers) hinges on how big a portion of the rent you give toward the down payment. If the amount is too small, the tenants won't value it and won't mind losing it. However, if it's big enough that the tenants can see their down payment accumulating right in front of their eyes, they will make the effort to buy rather than lose all that money.

Of course, you may be wondering about giving away a portion of the rent to the tenants. Doesn't that mean less money for you? Yes . . . and no.

To begin, remember that you're collecting the full rent each month (hopefully!) and you can use it toward paying your investment expenses (mortgage, taxes, insurance, maintenance, and so forth). You don't have to separately bank the amount that eventually goes toward the down payment. You can just give that as a credit to the buyers when they purchase.

Secondly, you can often charge a higher rent!

Yes, you can charge higher than market rent for a lease-option. Tenants-buyers are willing to pay more because they see it as part of a purchase, not just as a tenancy. For example, let's say that the market rent of your property is $1,000. You might be able to charge $1,200 rent on a lease-option. Then, if you credit the tenants with $400 a month toward the purchase, it's only really costing you $200. (The other $200 came from the inflated rental amount.)

TIP

Remember, the more credit you give the tenants-buyers toward the down payment, the better chance of a successful sale. If you make the credit too small, they may not buy.

Does a Lease-Option Have Risks?

It has one big downside. If the tenants begin to see that they won't be able to buy the property toward the end of the lease-option period, they may get resentful. They could, and many times do, abandon the property and leave it in bad shape.

Why do tenants do this?

Consider their position. The tenants are paying higher than market rent. (Tenants always know what the going rental rate is—don't think you can fool them!) The tenants are willing to put up with this because they know some of the money is going toward a down payment and toward the purchase of the property.

But what if half way through the rental period they begin to realize that the amount being put aside each month isn't nearly enough to cover their down payment (and, perhaps, some of the closing costs)? What if they begin to see that at the end of the agreement, they won't have enough money to make the purchase?

Then, they begin getting angry about that extra rental money they're paying. They see it going into the landlord's pocket and providing no benefit whatsoever to themselves. They begin to see the lease-option as a device that's taking advantage of them.

Many tenants in this position come to two realizations. The first is that they want out. So they abandon the property. This isn't bad for you in the sense that you at least get it back and can rent it again or do another lease-option.

The other realization, unfortunately, is that they want to get even. They want something in return for all that extra money they've paid each month that now won't be going toward the purchase. And they may take their anger out on the property not only by leaving it a mess, but causing serious damage.

TIP

Don't think that this won't happen. I have seen too many situations where the investors took back property from a failed lease-option and had to put thousands in to clean and repair it.

Can I Mitigate the Risk?

Of course you can. The way to reduce the risk of a failed lease-option, as noted earlier, is to increase the credit you give the tenant toward the purchase price. The more of the monthly rent that goes toward the purchase, the more likely that the tenant will be able to make the eventual purchase. And, as a result, the more likely the tenant will stick it out to a successful conclusion.

TIP

Don't be penny-wise and pound foolish. Don't try to grab most of that rent money for yourself. The more you give to the tenant, the more likely you are to have a successful lease-option that concludes in a sale.

Are There Any Other Risks?

The other risks are no more than you would face in any rental situation. The tenant could lose his or her job, be unable to make the rent payment, and leave. Or the tenants could have a divorce, or a medical problem, or even a death.

There are no certainties when renting and the same applies with a lease-option.

How Do I Qualify the Tenant-Buyer?

We've now come full circle back to finding the right person for the lease-option. Only now you know what you're looking for. You want someone who is basically cash poor but who can make substantial rental payments. You also want someone with good credit whom you can rely upon. But you don't want someone with impeccable credit who can get a little-to-nothing down mortgage and hence doesn't need you.

Does this person exist? Of course. You're most likely to find your target leasee-optionee in the form of a young couple just starting out in their twenties or perhaps thirties. Usually older people have accumulated some savings. Your best bet is to seek (advertise) for your tenant-buyer in areas where there are lots of apartment rentals.

TIP

Ask your would-be tenants-buyers to get a mortgage preapproval. This usually is available for just the cost of a credit check, typically under $50. It will show how big a mortgage/monthly loan payment they can afford. If it turns out they are nowhere near being able to qualify for a loan big enough to buy your property, you may want to pass on them.

Are There Additional Advantages to Using the Lease-Option?

We've already discussed some of the plusses, the biggest of which is that you lock in a buyer (or at least try to) as soon as you acquire the property. That means you don't have to go hunting later on. Here are some additional advantages.

Additional Advantages of a Lease-Option

- If you handle the work yourself, you won't need to hire an agent and pay a commission a few years later when it comes time to sell. This can be a substantial savings. On the other hand, you can hire an agent to find a lessee-optionee for you. But this will usually entail a rental fee and an eventual commission.

- You retain control. With a lease-option, the title to the property doesn't pass from you to the other party until the sale is actually concluded. Therefore, there is no chance for you to lose the property without getting your money (unless you agree to give the buyers a second mortgage, but that's another story).

- You usually don't have tax consequences (owe taxes) until the property actually sells (or the time period for the option runs out). For tax purposes, you handle the rental income in the same way you would for any other rental property. (Check with your professional tax advisor here.)

Are There Additional Disadvantages to Using the Lease-Option?

The biggest disadvantage we haven't discussed (we already talked about the tenant getting mad and leaving the place a mess) comes from the fact that you're locked into a sale.

Remember, the option is with the buyer, not with you. The lessee-optionee has the choice of going through with the purchase or not. *You don't have the choice of not selling.* If the tenants decide to buy, you MUST sell to them under the terms of the option.

What If I Change My Mind?

What if you give a three-year lease-option and at the end of that time you decide you'd rather hang onto the property than sell? If the tenants want to buy, you could try negotiating with them. You could even pay them money to not execute their option! However, if they were determined to purchase, they could demand that you sell and, if necessary, take you to court to force their rights.

What If There's a Price Inflation?

Another consideration is price increase. When you give an option it is normally for a certain price. You and the tenants might agree on the current value, or on some inflated value in the future. But, what if the price goes up substantially during the tenant's tenure? You could end up selling for below market!

Fortunately there is a solution here. A savvy investor will put an inflation clause into the lease-option. You'll sell for market price at the time the lease-option is given. But the clause says that the price will go up depending on a certain index. It could be keyed to overall inflation (which would have been a loser for you in recent years), or it could be keyed to the price increase in housing in your area as measured by some independent index (which would have been a winner for most sellers in recent years).

In this way you're protected from having to sell at a price lower than market.

TRAP

Savvy tenants-buyers who will go along with some sort of an inflation clause, often will also demand that it be reciprocal. In other words, yes they'll pay more if the price of the home increases. But, on the other side of the coin, they'll want to pay less if the price goes down! In other words, the price will be linked to the housing market up . . . or down.

Of course, this leads to yet another concern, namely that if the price of the property goes up too high, the tenants-buyers may not be able to afford a mortgage to buy it. But if that happens, you'll probably be so happy with your future profits that you won't mind!

20

Dodging the Tax Bullet

The old adage that the only two things you can't escape in life are death and taxes can be stretched a little bit. While there's no getting away from the grim reaper, you sometimes can keep the tax man at bay. It all depends on how you handle the sale of your property.

In this chapter we're going to look at some of the tax advantages of owning property. We'll also consider some perfectly legal strategies to keep from paying tax (or at least as large a tax) on your profit when you sell.

Special Note

The author is not engaged in providing tax advice. The following is simply an overview of tax rules affecting real estate investment property. For tax advice, consult with a tax professional.

Depreciation

If you own investment real estate, you can depreciate it. Depreciating means taking a certain percentage of its "cost" (we'll talk more about this later) each year as a reduction in value.

Almost all business assets can be depreciated. Cars, for example, are usually depreciated over a lifespan of five years. In a straight-line method, you might take 20 percent a year of the cost as a loss of value.

Rental real estate under current rules is depreciated over 27.5 years. Again, using a straight line method you would take 1/27.5 of the cost each year as a loss in value.

Of course, the value of property goes up, not down. So, how can you take a loss on an asset that's increasing in value? A helpful way to understand this is to think of it as a "paper loss." All assets deteriorate over time. Even a house will eventually fall away to dust. So instead of simply waiting until the end of its useful lifespan (arbitrarily decided by the government), you take a portion of the loss in value each year.

TIP

The time span of 27.5 years is specified by the government and is quite arbitrary. In the past, much shorter time spans have been allowed.

But, you may reasonably wonder, while the house will eventually deteriorate, the land never will. How do you depreciate land costs?

The answer is, you can't. You can only depreciate the building, not the land. The only exception would be if the land itself had an asset that was depletable, such as gas or oil.

Is Depreciation an Expense?

Yes it is. It's an expense much in the way that you have other expenses when you own rental property. For example, here's a list of some expenses you might expect to incur:

Typical Rental Property Expenses

- Mortgage interest
- Taxes
- Insurance
- Water service
- Garbage service
- Maintenance and repair
- Fix-up
- Advertising

- Pool and gardener service
- Depreciation

TIP

Save all your receipts! Unlike owning a house where the only deductions are typically property taxes and mortgage interest, with a rental property almost everything is deductible. You may even be able to deduct a phone, auto, even business cards! Check with your accountant.

When you add up all of the above expenses, you have the total expenses for your property over a month. Add all the monthlies together and that's how much it costs you over a year.

Now, subtract your total annual expenses from your total annual income, and that's your profit or loss.

Does Depreciation Contribute to Loss?

It certainly does. As soon as you begin to look at properties out there in the real world, you'll come to realize that finding one where the income comes even close to paying for the actual cash expenses is rare. When you add the paper loss of depreciation to your cash expenses, you almost always find that there's a loss.

Typical Income/Expense on a Rental House

Total annual income	$14,440	($1,200 monthly)
Total annual cash expenses	−14,000	
Positive cash flow	440	
Annual depreciation	−7,500	
Annual loss	−7,060	

Once depreciation is added in, you can almost always be assured that the property will show a loss, at least on paper. In our above example, a good property that actually shows a positive cash flow (more money coming in than cash expenses going out) turns into a big loser as soon as depreciation is added.

TIP

Remember, that the loss from depreciation is not an out-of-pocket expense. It's simply an accounting loss—it only shows up on paper.

In the dim past, depreciation was a tax dodge that was used by the wealthy to reduce their sizeable incomes. They would take that loss from real estate (that only occurred on paper) and deduct it from their ordinary income. That reduced their ordinary income and, of course, reduced the amount of taxes they would owe on that income.

That tax shelter was eliminated for the wealthy by the Tax Reform Act of 1986. Now it is only available if your income is less than $150,000. We'll have more to say about this shortly.

Depreciation Reduces the Tax Basis of the Property

Let's go back to when we were saying that depreciation reduced the "cost" of the building by a certain amount each year. While the cost is the most common method of establishing a tax basis, it's not the only consideration.

For tax purposes, there is a "basis" to each asset. That is the amount used for making tax calculations such as depreciation, or when you sell, for capital gains.

The basis, as we said, for most assets is their cost. However, with homes that basis can vary. For example, there are substantial transaction fees when you buy a home. Most of these are added to the basis.

Or, you may build an addition to the home. This is also added to the basis.

On the other hand, the basis may be reduced. Depreciation can reduce the basis of the property. Here's how it works:

Change in Basis Due to Depreciation

Original basis (cost)	$200,000
Add a room	+ 30,000
Adjusted basis	230,000
Depreciation ($7,000 annually for 10 years)	– 70,000
New adjusted basis	160,000

Notice that, although the property began with a basis of $200,000 which was its cost, the basis went up when a room was added, and more importantly here, went down when depreciation was calculated.

What's the Importance of the Tax Basis?

The reason that we've spent some time explaining basis is because it (and the sales price) determines the capital gains (and tax) you'll have to pay when you sell.

Your capital gain on the property is the difference between the adjusted tax basis and the sales price.

Calculating Capital Gain

Sales price (adjusted for costs of sale such as commission)	$300,000
Adjusted tax basis	– 160,000
Capital gain (on which tax is due)	140,000

Thus, to go through our example, you buy the property for $200,000, add a room for $30,000, which raises your basis, and then depreciate it for $70,000, which lowers the basis. When you sell, both the raising and lowering of the tax basis affects how big a capital gain you have.

TIP

It's important to keep one's eye on the donut and not the hole. What's important here is to see that depreciation can lower the basis, which means that upon sale there will be more capital gains (and resulting taxes).

All of which is to say that while depreciating real estate can produce a tax write-off, as noted earlier, when you sell, that tax loss all comes back to haunt you as a capital gain.

Thus, in decades past when anyone regardless of income could write off losses on real estate, what they were actually doing was converting their ordinary income to capital gains. Instead of paying high ordinary income taxes, they converted that income to a capital gain and paid lower capital gains taxes.

In case the above went by rather fast, let's take it again a bit slower. Let's consider just one year. In that year the property sustains a loss of $7,000 (primarily from depreciation). That $7,000 was then deducted from the investor's ordinary income. That meant that the investor avoided paying ordinary income taxes (read high tax rate) on $7,000.

The very next year that property sells, and it shows a $7,000 capital gain attributable to depreciation. The investor then had to pay tax on this amount. However, because it was a "capital gain" as opposed to "ordinary income," the tax rate was lower. Thus the great tax shelter benefit of real estate was that it converted ordinary income to capital gains and reduced the tax rate.

Doesn't That Work Now?

Not really, for two reasons. The first is that the Tax Reform Act of 1986 eliminated high-income investors from having the ability to take a deduction on their real estate losses. Then the Taxpayer Relief Act of 1997 reduced the capital gains rate (and added a few more wrinkles, as we'll shortly see).

To begin, however, let's consider the rules with regard to taking a loss from real estate as a deduction against your ordinary income.

Active Income

Tax law now discriminates between the types of income that we receive. Income from wages or as compensation for services is called Active Income. It includes commissions, consulting fees, salary, or anything similar. It's important for those involved in real estate to note that profits and losses from businesses in which you "materially participate" are included (not included are limited partnerships). However, activities from real estate are specifically excluded.

Passive Income

This is a bit trickier to define, but in general it means the profit or loss that we receive from a business activity in which we do not materially participate. This includes not only limited partnerships but also income from any real estate that is rented out. It's important to note that real estate is specifically defined as passive.

Portfolio Income

This is income from dividends, interest, royalties, and similar sources. We need not worry much about this here except to note that it does not include real estate income.

Under the old law, income was income and loss was loss. You could, thus, deduct any loss on real estate from your other income. Under the current law, your personal income is considered "active" while your real estate loss is considered "passive." Since you can't deduct a passive loss from active income, you can't, in general, write off real estate losses.

What About the Little Guy?

We've already said that these laws were primarily aimed at the wealthy to eliminate a big tax shelter. But there is an advantage to be retained here for the small investor.

There is an important exception to the above rule. This exception provides a $25,000 allowance for write offs for those with lower ordinary income. In other words, you can write off up to $25,000 in losses from real estate against your active income, provided you meet an income ceiling limitation (plus certain other qualifications).

Your Gross Adjusted Income Must Not Exceed $150,000

If your income is below $100,000, then you qualify for the entire $25,000 exception. If it is between $100,000 and $150,000, you lose fifty cents of the allowance for every dollar your income exceeds $100,000. The following chart will help explain this.

Phasing Out $25,000 Allowance as Income Increases

Income	Allowance	Income	Allowance	Income	Allowance
$100,000	$25,000	117,000	16,500	134,000	8,000
$101,000	24,500	118,000	16,000	135,000	7,500
$102,000	24,000	119,000	15,500	136,000	7,000
$103,000	23,500	120,000	15,000	137,000	6,500
$104,000	23,000	121,000	14,500	138,000	6,000
$105,000	22,500	122,000	14,000	139,000	5,500
$106,000	22,000	123,000	13,500	140,000	5,000
$107,000	21,500	124,000	13,000	141,000	4,500
$108,000	21,000	125,000	12,500	142,000	4,000
$109,000	20,500	126,000	12,000	143,000	3,500
$110,000	20,000	127,000	11,500	144,000	3,000
$111,000	19,500	128,000	11,000	145,000	2,500
$112,000	19,000	129,000	10,500	146,000	2,000
$113,000	18,500	130,000	10,000	147,000	1,500
$114,000	18,000	131,000	9,500	148,000	1,000
$115,000	17,500	132,000	9,000	149,000	500
$116,000	17,000	133,000	8,500	150,000	0

Since most small investors have incomes under $150,000, the allowance applies to them. They can deduct their losses on real estate up to the $25,000 limitation.

What's the Other Qualification?

You'll recall that we said there was another qualification. It is that you must actively participate in the business of renting the property.

This can be tricky. After all, what does "actively participate" really mean?

Obviously if you own the property and are the only person directly involved in handling the rental—meaning that you advertise it, rent it, handle maintenance and clean up, collect the rent, etc.—then you materially participate.

However, there are gray zones. Generally if you don't personally determine the rental terms, approve new tenants, sign for repairs, or approve capital improvements and the like, then you may not qualify.

The question always comes up, "What if I hire a management firm to handle the property for me?"

This is even grayer. In general, a management firm is probably okay to use as long as you continue to materially participate (determine rental terms, approve new tenants, sign for repairs or capital improvements, and the like). If you are going to use a management firm, be sure that you have your attorney check over the agreement you sign with the firm to see that it does not characterize you as not materially participating and thus prevent you from deducting any loss.

Are There Any Other Kinks in the Rules?

On the surface, the allowance and the qualifications may seem straightforward. But, they can be tricky. For example, here are some other considerations:

1. The income used to determine whether you qualify is your gross adjusted income. This means your income after you have taken some deductions such as retirement plan contributions (not IRAs), alimony, moving expenses, and others.

2. The allowance does not apply to farms. If you materially participate in the running of a farm, other rules apply—see your accountant or tax attorney.

3. Those who don't qualify for taking the deduction against their active income, cannot likewise take the deduction against their portfolio income. (Remember, portfolio income came from interest, dividends, royalties, etc.)

So, When I Sell, Chances Are I Will Owe Some Capital Gains?

Yes, assuming you don't sell for a loss. However, as noted, the capital gains tax rate has been reduced. At the present time it's a maximum of 25 percent for long-term gains. Hence, even if you do have to pay, it won't be a confiscatory amount.

TRAP

You owe tax on a capital gain regardless of whether the property is investment or personal residence. However, if you sell at a capital loss, while you can take that loss on investment property, you can't take a deduction against that loss if it's on a personal residence! A quirk in the tax laws.

Is There Any Legal Way of Avoiding a Tax on My Profits?

That, of course, is the national pastime that most Americans play—how to legally avoid paying high taxes. And, in the case of investment real estate, there are a few loopholes that can benefit the investor.

The first method which might be used is to convert the property from an investment to a personal residence. You can remove the tenants and move in yourself, declaring the property your principal residence. After a period of time, you may then be able to sell the home and reap the benefits of the principal residence capital gains exclusion of up to $500,000.

TIP

Keep in mind that in real estate you only owe taxes on your profit (capital gain) when you sell. No matter how high the value of your property goes, you don't pay tax on it as long as you continue to own it. (You would, of course, owe income taxes if you showed excess income over expenses on an annual basis.)

There are certain problems with the above scenario, however. The first is, how long must you reside in the property to make it your personal residence? I don't know of any hard and fast rule. Some accountants say two years, others longer. Check with your professional tax advisor.

The second has to do with all that depreciation taken while you owned the property. Under current rules, it is recaptured at a special rate. Thus, even though you may avoid paying taxes on most of your capital gain by using the personal property exclusion (noted below), you might still owe some taxes on the recaptured depreciation losses that you took earlier.

TIP

Yet another problem here is that very often the investor is not really interested in moving into the rental property. In that case, a tax-deferred exchange, as described below, might be better.

How Does the Up-to-$500,000 Exclusion Work?

Under the 1997 Taxpayer Relief Act, each person regardless of age can exclude up to $250,000 of the capital gain on a principle residence. For a couple, that multiplies up to $500,000.

TIP

The exclusion can only be taken on a principle residence. It CANNOT be taken on investment property unless that investment property was previously converted to a principle residence.

There are some fine print rules involved in the exclusion that your professional tax advisor can explain to you, but the big rule to keep in mind is that in order to obtain the exclusion, you must have lived in the property for two of the previous five years.

That means two things: first, you have to live in the property (not just own it) for two years before you can claim the exclusion. Second, you can only claim the exclusion once every two years. Thus, if you own 15 rental properties, it would take you 30 years at minimum to bail out of all of them in this fashion!

Is There Another Way of Legally Avoiding Paying Taxes on My Capital Gain?

Yes, there is. You can trade your property for another and defer the capital gain from the old property to the new. This is technically called a "like kind" Internal Revenue Code Section 1031 Tax-Deferred Exchange.

A great many investors see this as a means of multiplying their profits without paying taxes along the way. They hopscotch from property to property, increasing the value of their real estate holdings unencumbered by paying taxes for each transaction.

TIP

It's sort of like getting compound interest on your equity. Normally, in a strict sale followed by a purchase of another property, you would pay taxes on your capital gain. That would leave you less equity to invest in the next property. However, by deferring that tax bill into the future, you have all your equity to put into the next property, meaning you can buy a bigger and better investment house!

The rules for a tax-free exchange were greatly simplified over a decade ago by several tax cases, the most famous of which is called the "Starker rule." Under Starker, you just go ahead and sell your investment property as you would otherwise. However, you then have a qualified intermediary, such as the trust department of a bank or title insurance company, hold your money. You now have 45 days after the sale to designate a new property into which you will invest your money. And you have 180 days to close the deal on that new property.

Note that there are other strict conditions of the exchange which must be met. The new property must be equal or of greater value than the old. Another is that you may not normally take cash ("boot") as part of the sale. If you want cash out, you must usually refi the old property before the exchange, or refi the new property after the exchange. Again, check with your accountant for details.

Another condition is that only like kinds of properties can be exchanged. In our case, that means exchanging for another property held for investment or use in business or trade. It would not mean that you could exchange for a personal residence.

Can I Combine an Exchange and a Personal Property Exclusion?

One of the problems we noted earlier with converting an investment property into a personal property was that you may not want to reside in a property you own as an investment. If that's the case, then the answer could be simple. Just do a tax-deferred exchange of the investment property into one in which you would like to live. Then at a later date convert the desirable home from investment to principal residence.

Keep in mind, however, the "like kind" rule noted above. A personal residence is not the same as an investment house. Therefore, in order to not invalidate the tax-deferred status of the exchange, you would have to rent out the new property for a time before moving in yourself. How long do you have to rent it before converting it to a personal residence? Some tax advisors have suggested six months, others as long as two years or more. Again, check with your professional tax advisor.

Keep Good Records

From our discussion here, one other thing should be apparent: you need to keep good records. It's very important that you keep every receipt and note every expense and piece of income in a ledger.

You may have to prove to the IRS that expenses you had on your investment property were real. For example, three years earlier you might have had a vacancy, and you spent $115 advertising to get a new tenant.

Prove it, says the IRS. So, you reach into your bag of receipts and pull out an invoice from the local paper for $115 for advertising. Attached to it is a copy of the ad itself and your check in payment. There's no disputing that.

Also, keep all records if you make improvements to the property. Remember, improvements RAISE the tax basis which will later reduce the amount of capital gains you will need to pay. (The higher the tax basis, the less the capital gain.)

If you make a capital improvement, such as a new roof or patio, keep all of the receipts. At the end of the year your accountant will be able to use them to adjust your tax basis upward.

TIP

Just because you spend money improving your rental, doesn't mean that you've made a capital improvement for tax purposes. Replacing a water heater, for example, is not a capital improvement, it's a repair. Adding a tile roof where there was previously a less expensive tar roof would be a capital improvement (of at least the difference in price between the tar roof and the tile).

What If I Refinance?

As strange as it may seem, refinancing your property without a sale has no immediate tax consequences. You don't report new mortgages to the IRS. You will, however, have less equity to rely upon later if any capital gains taxes are due when you sell.

If I have conveyed nothing else to you in this chapter, I hope that I have at least given the impression that buying and selling real estate goes hand in hand with tax considerations. If you're a wise investor, you'll consult with your tax professional each time before you make a new move.

21
The Real Estate
Money Tree

The dream of acquiring wealth is as old as America itself. While some of the original settlers came to this country to avoid religious persecution, many, particularly the plantation owners of the South, came here to get rich.

That combined dream of freedom and acquiring wealth has played out through the history of the country. John Jacob Astor built his wealth in New York City by acquiring real estate ahead of growth, waiting for the city to catch up, and then selling for profit. The railroad barons acquired wealth not by bridging the continent with trains, but by acquiring vast real estate alongside the railroad right-of-way. The majority of today's wealthy, whether they acquired their assets through stock investment, business entrepreneurship, or by buying and selling property, hold much (if not most) of that wealth in the form of real estate.

In short, if you aspire to make your fortune in real estate, you're not alone. You're part of a strong national tradition. And chances are you'll succeed! The number of Americans today who own big stakes real estate is in the many millions.

What Is a Real Estate
Money Tree?

In this book we've looked at two methods of building your fortune in property: flipping to get cash out quickly, and holding for a time before reselling at a profit. Now I'd like to turn to one last method which I call "The Real Estate Money Tree."

217

My father was actually the person who named this process. He believed in it completely and worked at it his entire life.

The idea is really quite simple. You acquire properties (single-family homes, condos, small strip malls, . . . whatever) slowly, one at a time. You buy, but you never sell. Over time you acquire a vast holding in real estate.

It's this latter strategy which differentiates this plan from anything we've discussed thus far. It's holding real estate for holding's sake.

Perhaps you know someone who has done this (many people have). Typically they lead quiet lives and are not ostentatious. You may have several in your neighborhood. Many have regular jobs, but most who are successful, devote their time to taking care of their properties. They are the most busy at the first of the month when they go around "harvesting." That is, collecting their rents.

You see, over time the mortgages on these properties get paid off. When they are originally purchased, the mortgage may be very high, often 95 percent of the purchase price or more. (These investors often live in the properties they buy for a time before converting them to rentals, thus qualifying for the high loan-to-value mortgage.) However, over 30 years that mortgage gets reduced to zero. Now the investor has a paid off rental and most of the rent money goes into his or her pocket.

Some investors literally have hundreds of properties. Of course, once that happens they tend to hire good property management firms to take care of the rentals.

Most such investors, however, have around a dozen such properties—and they take care of them by themselves. (A dozen paid off properties bringing in an average of $1,200 a month is $14,400—not a bad monthly income! Twelve properties with an average price of $250,000 comes to $3 million, again not a bad net worth!)

TIP

The principle is simple—you buy properties and rent them out to make the payments. Eventually you pay them off and live off the income they generate.

The money tree plan appeals to many people because of its simplicity. You don't have to be a genius to make it work. Indeed, all you need do is keep your eyes open for good properties and purchase them as you can. Here are the details.

Should I Buy Break-Even Properties Only?

While it may seem simple enough in concept, unless you buy right, you could go down in flames using the money tree concept. The last thing in the world you want is a bunch of alligators, properties that eat at you rather than feed you. Since you're going to hold these properties for a very long time, it is crucial that right from the start they be at break-even or close to it. Buying properties with big negative cash flows is a no-no. You might be able to handle one or even two. But acquire more and you'll simply be overwhelmed by the cash drain.

But, you may reasonably wonder, how do you acquire properties with close to positive cash flow in an era when prices are accelerating?

It's simple . . . wait for the right property to show up. The beauty of this plan is that it doesn't require you to take precipitous action. You have a lifetime to buy your properties. As long as you're always out there looking, sooner or later you'll come across a suitable deal. It may take several months. In a tight market, it could even take a year or more. But it will happen. When you see the good deal (a break-even property), acquire it.

TIP

Remember, the real estate market (like all markets) is cyclical. If the market's hot, wait. It will cool down and buying opportunities will abound. As long as you're not out there to make a quick killing, you have the time to wait it out. Buy only when prices are reasonable and a rental break-even is possible.

Should I Buy Young Properties?

This is an important concept, one that too few people who do the money tree thing catch onto. And while things may go well at first, they must pay the toll later on.

Buildings, all buildings, have a limited lifespan. While it may not seem that way at any given point, it's a fact. A 25-year-old house may seem perfectly sound today. However, in another 25 years it may be falling down and requiring all sorts of costly repairs. A 50-year-old house may seem like a bargain, after it's fixed up. But what's it going to cost you to refurbish it when it's 75 years old?

The key to buying property long term is to buy that property when it's young, no more than 10 years old. That way as you grow old gracefully, so will your real estate. Twenty-five years from now, with the proper maintenance, the house should still be in reasonably good shape and should still be producing a healthy rental income.

What About Where to Buy?

Neighborhoods change. Sometimes, not always, today's blue-collar or white-collar neighborhood will become tomorrow's slum. If you buy into a neighborhood that turns sour, you'll own a home in an area where you may eventually be afraid to go and collect the rent!

You need to buy in sound neighborhoods, ones that will remain solid year after year. But how do you identify this type of neighborhood?

Quite frankly, short of having a crystal ball, no one can know for sure what will happen to a neighborhood 25 years down the road. However, some things tend to remain constant. If the neighborhood is near good schools and shopping and "looks good" with lots of trees and landscaping; if it's away from industry, commercial settings, and heavily trafficked streets; and most importantly, if it's recognized as a "good neighborhood" when you buy, then chances are it will remain so for a long time to come.

When you're buying short term, you can ignore a neighborhood problem, such as a large commercial center or run-down homes a few streets over. But you can't ignore such things when you buy long term.

TIP

When you buy for the long term, the neighborhood must be all pluses with no negatives.

Should I Keep My Day Job?

Remember, this is not a get-rich-quick-scheme. When you get started, there will be little to no cash flow from the properties. Instead, they will be like little plants which require constant nurturing. You'll have to take money out-of-pocket to pay for maintenance and repair . . . and occasionally to offset some mortgage and tax payments.

Of course, as we saw in the chapter on taxation, you may get some immediate tax relief. Or, depending on your income you may not. It is for this reason that you should plan on continuing to do whatever it is you do for a living.

Additionally many investors begin by moving into their investment house initially. As a principal residence they can deduct their property taxes and mortgage interest. And, they can fix up the property while they stay there.

TIP

Many "Money Tree" investors begin by converting their principal residence to a rental, buying another home to live in, converting it, and continuing on in the same fashion, never selling their last home.

Of course, you may be wondering how on earth you'll get the down payment for the next home without selling the previous one? We discussed "bridge" and "gap" financing in Chapter 14. This is a different approach.

How Do I Get Cash Out?

Earlier we spoke of "harvesting" your real estate Money Tree by collecting rents. There's yet another way of harvesting your properties: refinancing.

Two things happen as you own a property over time. The first is that prices go up. This is a function of supply and demand as well as inflation (see the Appendix if you don't believe this). Buy a property, hold it five years, and chances are it will be worth considerably more than you paid for it (assuming you didn't happen to buy at the beginning of a rare down cycle!).

The other thing is that your mortgage balance goes down, albeit slowly. Each month as you make that payment, a small amount of money is returned to equity. During the first 10 years of ownership, that amount tends to be small. But after the 10th year, it accelerates, until by the 25th year almost the entire payment is going back to equity (assuming a 30-year mortgage).

This means that you can "harvest" this property by refinancing to get money out. For example, if you bought a property for $150,000 with a $140,000 mortgage, and that property goes up in price to $200,000, you've now got $60,000 in equity. If the mortgage goes down to $120,000, your equity is now $80,000. You can cash out some of that equity.

A few years ago lenders frowned on giving cash-out mortgages to investors. Indeed, the most you were likely to get was a 70 percent mortgage. If you got anything higher, the proceeds had to go to pay off the existing mortgage and costs. No cash outs were allowed.

Today that's changed. Many of today's lenders will allow a cash out to you on an 80 percent mortgage, in some cases on as high as a 90 percent mortgage. (Shop around with the help of a good mortgage broker to find these loans.)

This means that when you refinance to an 80 percent mortgage, in our above example, you could get $160,000, meaning you could cash out $40,000 on the property. With a 90 percent loan, that's $60,000 cash out to you, quite a nice harvest!

Keep in mind that because you're not changing title, only refinancing, there are no immediate tax consequences. Indeed, as long as you hold the property there won't be any tax consequences. Thus, you can do anything you want with the money you cash out, including using it to buy another home!

Buy one property, hold it a few years, get cash out, and buy another home. Now you've got two. Hold them a few years, get cash out, and buy two more homes. Now you've got four. Keep repeating the process and it won't be too many years before you yourself are a land baron!

My father acquired many properties over his lifetime and he would always speak of them as money trees. When he needed money to buy another property (or for any reason), he would simply refinance.

TRAP

In order to refinance you must show income, another reason, at least in the early years, to keep your day job!

Are There Any Drawbacks?

When I've first explained the concept of a real estate money tree to people, often they would remark that it's so obvious, why didn't they think of it? Indeed, it is obvious and simple. However, there are some potential drawbacks that you should be aware of.

The first is that it works best if you start young. Then you have many years to acquire property. If you start near retirement age, you will still be able to acquire a number of properties, but you will find that you're going to need to nurture these young ventures just when you want to get money out to retire. For those nearing retirement age, a better plan is the buy, rent, and sell described in earlier chapters of this book.

The other concern is that, as we've noted in many places, real estate is cyclical. And if you simply buy and hold indefinitely, you're really not taking advantage of the cycles.

One of the things that I do different than my father did, is to sell when prices accelerate and then buy back other properties when prices fall.

Of course, this can be a risky strategy. If you miss the top or the bottom by a large amount it can be costly. On the other hand, if you guess right, you can clear significant profits on your properties, much more than simply by holding on indefinitely.

TIP

It's a myth that the price of real estate always goes up. Since the Second World War it's declined on at least four occasions, the most significant being the real estate recession of the early 1990s.

Should I Do It?

The bottom line is that the money tree works, and works well. If you're conservative, and if you have the time to grow old with your properties, they will take wonderful financial care of you.

Appendix

Why Inflation Is Your Friend

A few years ago there was a popular movie called, Back to the Future. In Part III of that movie the hero, Michael J. Fox, goes back to 1885 and there, with the help of co-star Christopher Lloyd, gets a time machine to work, thus bringing him back to the future.

It was a good movie. But as I was watching it I kept asking myself, "How did he buy anything back then?"

It's one thing to take a time machine to the past. It's quite another to buy a hat or a pair of shoes or parts to fix a time machine in 1885. How did he buy anything?

This is not to say that things were expensive out West back then. A bath and a shave were probably 7 cents. A night at a hotel 20 cents. A meal might cost a dime and so forth. Things cost very little. But what did our hero pay for them with? I don't think merchants back then accepted Visa, American Express, or Master Card.

Today's paper money wouldn't have done very well back in 1885 either. It wouldn't be recognized or accepted, since there was virtually no paper money of any kind in the old West in those days.

Did they take back pocket change? Our "silver" coins are all virtually worthless, shiny base metal. Can you imagine a western saloonkeeper in 1885 accepting a clad quarter (made of copper and nickel) in payment for a "slug of whiskey"? He'd bite the coin, determine it wasn't silver or gold, and throw the person who offered it out the door.

So, how did our heroes buy anything?

Making Purchases in 1885

The answer is real money. For example, Michael J. Fox could have used pennies . . . not pennies from today, but pennies from 1885.

In 1885 the accepted penny across the country was the Indian head. (It was the precursor to our current Lincoln cent.) If our heroes had the foresight to get a roll of Indian head pennies before they went to the past, they probably could have done very well. One roll of pennies would undoubtedly have bought them everything they needed for several days. If they happened to pick up a "double eagle" ($20 gold piece) of the period, they'd have enough money to live royally for a week or more.

Think of it . . . a penny actually buying something substantial instead of just weighing down your pocket with unwanted change. Twenty dollars lasting weeks! Our heroes could have lived like royalty for next to nothing.

Well, not quite.

The truth of the matter is that they just couldn't go to a bank today and simply ask for, "Indian head cents, please." Or, "I'll have a $20 gold piece." Even though those items are still authorized currency of the United States, they are available only from collectors and rare coin dealers who keep track of true value. A single Indian head cent in even modestly good condition might cost 10 of today's dollars. A common date $20 gold piece could be close to 800 current dollars.

When comparing prices of yesterday with the present, this is the part of the story that is often overlooked. Not only did things cost far less in the past, but the very money that was used to purchase them in the past costs far more today.

In short, many things from the past that survive to the present actually retain their original buying power. Rare coins are one good example. Real estate is another.

A Piece of History

When you buy a resale house or small apartment rental, you're buying a piece of the past. You're buying an item that was built 1, 3, 7, or even 47 years ago.

When you compare today's price of that older structure with the price it cost brand new, you will find almost invariably that it costs more today in actual dollars than it did back then. Just like a bath or a meal or a room from 1885, the house built 10 years ago costs far more to purchase today than it did years earlier.

However, like the Indian head pennies or the double eagle $20 gold piece, that house retains its value through time. In terms of "buying power," the dollars you receive for that house today, even in a depressed market, will buy as much if not more than they did in the past when the house was first built.

Money's Loss of Value

Let's look at it from a different angle. Instead of considering that which retains buying power, such as a house, let's consider for a few moments that which loses buying power: money.

No reasonable person will argue that the value of the dollar has declined. There are many reasons for this decline, including the increasing size of our money supply, the nation's borrowing—in the form of the national debt and foreign trade debt, and the real or controlled scarcity of certain commodities such as oil. However, no matter what the reason, the simple fact is that consistently since the founding of our country, our money has become worth less and less in terms of what it will buy. To say it another way, it takes more and more money to buy the same item. (Of course, it hasn't been a steady decline. There have been periods of relative stability interspersed with periods of strong decline.)

The government even attempts to measure the overall decline of our currency. Each month the federal government releases the "Consumer Price Index" (CPI) and the "Wholesale Price Index" (WPI) which purport to measure the loss in buying power of the dollar when compared with the previous 1-month and 12-month periods.

TIP

Don't trust what the government says in the CPI and WPI. Inflation is usually much higher. A few years ago when housing prices started moving upward very dramatically, they skewed the inflation indices. Higher housing prices pushed the CPI rate into double digits. In response to this, the government removed the price of buying a house from the CPI and instead substituted the cost of renting, at the time a much lower and steadier figure. Thus the CPI could show a much lower level of inflation (although a false one if you happened to be buying a house).

The Unseen Effects of Inflation

All of which is to say that something which hasn't changed in a very long time (certainly since 1885, and a lot before then) isn't likely to change in the future. Inflation has been a steady companion since the birth of our country and it's likely going to be with us for a long time in the future. Except for relatively short periods (such as during the Great Depression), it's a constant that we need to accept and deal with.

The problem is that it has become unfashionable to speak of inflation. Back in 1980 when the government's CPI showed inflation to be running at an annual rate of 12 percent, it was on everyone's lips. Recently, however, with it running around 2 or 3 percent, few people worry about it. Mention inflation and many people will yawn. They've already heard that story.

But although 5 percent inflation is a lot less than 12 percent, it is still an enormous rate, and it can have an immense impact on pricing, particularly in real estate.

The Rule of 72

To see how inflation works in housing prices, let's use the "rule of 72." In case you're not familiar with it, the rule of 72 allows you to determine how quickly your money will double at any given interest rate. You just divide the interest rate into 72 and that gives the number of years that it takes to double your money. For example, at 10 percent interest, your money doubles in 7.2 years. At 4 percent interest it takes 18 years, and so forth.

We can also use the rule of 72 for inflation. If the rate of inflation is 6 percent, then our money will lose half its value in 12 years (12 × 6 = 72). If the rate of inflation is 5 percent, it will take 14.4 years to lose half its value (14.4 × 5 = 72).

Since the end of World War II, the rate of inflation in the United States has averaged around 5 to 6 percent. That means that every 12 to 15 years, our money loses half its value. A 2001 dollar, in other words, is worth about 10 cents in terms of the buying power of a 1946 dollar. To put it another way, you need around 10 of today's dollars to equal the buying power of 1 dollar back in 1946.

Now, what does this say for real estate?

The long-term trend in inflation in this country means that when a house costs a $250 million today, it isn't as much money as most of us suppose. Today, $250,000 is only about $25,000 in 1946 dollars. It's not just that houses have gone up in price because of shortages and increased demand (they have), it's also because of the fact that our money is simply worth less and it takes more of it to buy the same amount.

The Hilly Rose Show

Is $200,000 (about the median cost of a house) really not a lot of money?

Let me answer that question with a short, true story. Back in 1976 I was a guest on a talk radio show out of Los Angeles, the Hilly Rose show. I can still remember the host asking me in consternation, "How can the price of a house go higher?" At the time, the average price for a house in the city was going for around $70,000, a seemingly incredible figure. It seemed obvious to him, as it was to most people, that prices simply couldn't go up.

I answered him in a single word, inflation.

I don't think he believed me. But he should have. Try to buy any house in L.A. for $70,000 today!

Buying Power

Consider again the film *Back to the Future*. When Michael J. Fox was in 1885, what could he have brought back to the present that would have made him rich beyond his wildest dreams?

Obviously he could have bought back some Indian pennies and sold them for 10 current dollars apiece. Or he could have brought back $20 gold pieces and sold them for 800 current dollars.

But what he could have brought back that would have made him even more fabulously wealthy is a deed. He could have brought back a deed to property in downtown Denver or San Francisco. He could

have brought back a deed to virtually any piece of property anywhere, bought then for perhaps $100 or less, which would sell today
for hundreds of thousands, if not millions, of dollars. Can you imagine what any piece of property bought in 1885 would be worth today
. . . anywhere at all in the country?!

It's really from the perspective of the past that the true value of
real estate, in this case investment, becomes clear. If property
bought in 1885 would be considered to be worth a fortune today,
can it be any less true for property bought today when considered
100 years from now? Fifty years? Ten?

As long as we continue to have inflation and our money continues
to be worth less and less, real estate will be worth more and more. It
helps if shortages of housing drives prices up, but it really doesn't
matter. It helps if there's increased demand from a growing population, but it really doesn't matter. It helps if construction materials
cost more, but it really doesn't matter. The only thing that really
matters is inflation. As long as there's inflation, housing will increase
in value. And it doesn't look as though inflation is going away anytime soon. (Two hundred years of inflation can't be wrong.)

TIP

Don't be intimidated by price. It's much like clothing.
Most people aren't aware that today's formal clothing
is really the day-to-day business clothing of the last
generation. Similarly most of the prices that we use to
judge by are the prices the last generation paid for
things. Keep up to date. Higher prices today are, in
most cases, simply a reflection of inflation, of the
declining buying power of our currency. Don't fall
into the trap of believing that prices could never go
higher. They always do.

Housing Shortages

Most of us look around and see homes everywhere. How can there
be a housing shortage when there are so many houses and apartments and condos?

To answer that question, just remember that houses don't last forever. The actual life span of a single-family dwelling is estimated by builder organizations to be between 50 and 80 years. That means that residential units built before about 1920 to 1950 (as of this writing) are reaching the end of their useful life.

Of course, such buildings can be refurbished and modernized. You can see this happening in the fashionable areas of nearly every city from New York to San Francisco. But for every one older building that is preserved, there are 10 that are either bulldozed to the ground or are virtually uninhabitable. To see these you have only to travel through the vast ghettos and blighted areas of virtually every American city.

When you compare the number of decaying residential properties (single-family and apartments) that are ending their useful life to the number of new properties being built, you quickly find that in most areas of the country, the new is not keeping up with the decline of the old.

Add to this the enormous influx of immigrants that have come to the United States over the past several decades, not to mention our population growth just from the birth rate, and it's easy to see that the demand for housing is incredibly strong.

Further, keep in mind that during the real estate recession of 1990 to about 1997, relatively few housing units were built. That means that not only are we not keeping up, but we have a deficit to overcome from the last decade.

All of which is to say that housing demand is not going to diminish anytime soon. What will diminish is the public's ability to afford housing as prices get higher. But that will only slow, not stop, the great rush to housing in this country.

The Bottom Line

All of which is to say that you don't have to be smart to buy right in real estate. You don't have to spend months finding the right property (although that will increase your profits faster). You don't even need a plan! All you need to do is to get into the market and wait. Over time, inflation and housing shortages will build your real estate fortune for you!

Index

Accountants, professional tax advice from, 175, 212
Active income, 208, 210–211
Age of property, 68–69, 94–95, 101, 141–142, 219–220
Alienation clause, 22, 130–132, 135
"Alligators," 7–8, 167–175
Annual return, price appreciation and, 5–6
Appliance fix–up costs, 142
Appraisal manipulation, 23, 85–86
"As is" properties, 78, 82, 83, 84, 91
Assignment, 16–22
Attorneys:
    buying at foreclosure sales and, 62–63
    eviction proceedings and, 84, 164–165, 181–182
Auction, buying at, 62–63
Automatic sprinklers, 144

Bank accounts, for investment property, 168–169
Bankruptcy, eviction and, 165
Bathroom fix–up costs, 183, 184
Bedrooms, number of, 143
Birds, 157
Bonuses, repos and, 88
Bookkeeping system, 168–171
Boot, 214
Bridge loans, 128
Buyer manipulation, 23, 85–86

Capital gains, 175, 211–215
    exclusion of residence from, 115–116, 212–215
    tax basis and, 207–208, 215–216
Carpeting and pad fix–up costs, 79, 183, 184
Cash reserves, 45–46, 114, 115

Cats, 157
Children, 143, 156
Clean–up costs:
    determining, 78–79, 145–146
    in evictions, 165
    importance of clean rental property, 78–79, 145–146, 151–152
    security/cleaning deposits and, 158–159, 163, 194
Close–in locations, 67–68
Closing costs, 5–6, 81
CMA (Comparative Market Analysis), 34–35, 40–41
Co–ops, as investment properties, 27, 112, 142–143
Cold markets, flipping in, 13
Commingling funds, 168
Commissions, real estate, 185, 186, 199
Commuting times, 67–68
Condominiums, as investment properties, 26–27, 90, 91, 142–143
Contingencies:
    in assignment, 17–19
    for Fannie Mae repos, 91
    for handyman specials, 98–99
Conversion to rental, 111–118, 221
    buying to convert, 127
    determining wisdom of, 111–113
    equity conversion in, 113–114
    monthly payments in, 114–115
    steps in, 116–118
    tax consequences of, 115–116
Cosmetic specials, 96–97
Counter fix–up costs, 183, 184
Counter–offers, 41, 42, 98
"Cows," 167–175
Creative financing, 34, 44, 99–100, 129–136
Credit card financing, 101

Credit rating:
   determining, 124–125
   foreclosure and, 130
   of potential tenants, 154–155
Customs Department repos, 92

Delayed purchase (*see* Lease–options)
Deposits:
   liquidated damages clause and, 19–20
   security/cleaning, 158–159, 163, 194
Depreciation, 203–211
   deductibility of, 8, 115, 168, 174–175,
      206, 208–211
   recapture of, 213
   and tax basis of property, 206–208,
      215–216
Disclosure (*see* Full disclosure)
Dogs, 157
Door and door handle fix–up costs, 79
Double escrow, 21–22, 50
Down payment:
   annual return and, 5–6
   on conversion to rental, 113
   creative financing and, 133–135
   on investment properties, 6, 44–45,
      121–124
   in lease–options, 195–198
Driveway, 182
Duplexes, as investment properties, 27

Electrical fix–up costs, 79, 141
Equifax, 124
Escape clauses (*see* Contingencies)
Escrow:
   double, avoiding, 21–22, 50
   in flipping, 14
   real estate options and, 15
Eviction proceedings, 158, 163,
     164–165, 181–182
Expense analysis, 32–33
   cutting expenses, 171–173
   maintenance expenses, 7–8, 32–33,
     126, 172
   other expenses, 33
   PITI (Principal, Interest, Taxes,
     Insurance), 7, 32
   vacancy expense, 7–8, 33, 114, 126

Expenses, bookkeeping for, 169–171
Experion, 124

Fair Isaac (FICO), 124–125
Fannie Mae, 90–91, 124
"Farming for bargains," 105–106
Federal Deposit Insurance Corporation
   repos, 92
Fencing fix–up costs, 79
FHA (Federal Housing
   Administration), 86–88, 101, 135
FICO (Fair Isaac), 124–125
Financial profiling, 122, 124–125
Financing, 121–136
   bridge loans, 128
   creative, 34, 44, 99–100, 129–136
   credit card, 101
   finance contingency and, 18–19
   in flipping, 127–128, 129–133
   gap loans, 128
   of handyman specials, 100–101
   home equity loans, 46, 101
   personal loans, 128
   refinancing, 7, 9, 113, 172, 216,
     221–222
   seller, 34, 44, 99–100, 129–136
   (*See also* Mortgages)
Fix–up costs:
   determining, 78–79, 184–185
   for handyman specials, 94–97, 100
   neighborhood norms and, 183
   recordkeeping for, 215–216
   for REOs, 81
   for repos, 88
   second opinions and, 184
   in selling a rental, 182–185
Flats, as investment properties, 27
Flipping, 6–7, 11–23
   assignment in, 16–22
   contract of sale in, 132–133
   daring foreclosure in, 130–132
   described, 11–12
   extent of, 12–13
   financing in, 127–128, 129–133
   of government repos, 85–86
   holding versus, 24, 29
   manipulation in, 23, 85–86

Flipping (*Cont.*)
  mechanics of, 13–14
  neighborhood analysis and, 28
  real estate brokers and, 21–22, 50, 86
  real estate options in, 14–16
  rules for, 12
  second mortgages in, 22–23
Foreclosure, 53–63
  agents and, 55
  buying at auctions, 62–63
  costs of righting, 58–62
  daring, in flipping process, 130–132
  judicial, 131
  lender, 57 (*See also* Government
    repos; REOs)
  locating properties in, 54–57, 62–63
  mechanics of, 53–54
  motivated sellers and, 51
  newspaper notices of, 56
  owner, 54–55, 57–62
  reasons for, 54
Foundations, 96, 97
Freddie Mac, 91–92, 124
Front walkway, 182
FSBOs (For Sale By Owner):
  rental properties, 185, 186–188
  signs, 54–55
  Website listings, 103, 107–109, 187
Full disclosure:
  in assignment, 20–22
  disclosure contingency and, 18–19
  in flipping, 12
  lack of, with REOs, 82
  in selling a rental, 188–189

Gap loans, 128
Gardening services, 153, 172,
    173
General Services Administration (GSA)
    repos, 92
Government repos, 85–92
  Fannie Mae, 90–91
  flipping, 85–86
  Freddie Mac, 91–92
  HUD (Housing and Urban
    Development Department),
    86–88

Government repos (*Cont.*)
  other programs, 92
  VA (Veteran's Administration),
    88–90

Handyman specials, 93–102
  contingencies for, 98–99
  deciding what to repair in, 100
  identifying, 94–97
  offers for, 98–100
  REOs as, 77–79
  repos as, 88, 89
  selling, 101–102
  special financing for, 100–101
Highway infrastructure, 67–68
Holding, 23–24, 218
  creative financing of, 135–136
  flipping versus, 24, 29
  long–term, 135–136
  minimizing costs of, 24
Home equity loans, 46, 101
Homeowner's associations (HOAs), 27,
    112, 142–143
Housing and Urban Development
    Department (HUD), repos of,
    86–88

Inflation:
  impact of, 225–231
  lease–options and, 200–201
Inspection (*see* Professional home
    inspection)
Insurance expense, 7, 32, 144–145,
    170, 172
Interest expense, 32
Interest rate:
  for investors versus owner–occu-
    pants, 123–124
  points and, 122–123
Internal Revenue Service (IRS), 92,
    168
  (*See also* Taxes)
Internet, 103–109
  agent listings, 103, 104, 107–108
  "farming for bargains" and, 105–106
  FSBO (For Sale By Owner) listings,
    103, 107–109, 187

Internet (*Cont.*)
 government agency Website listings,
  87, 89, 91, 92
 pros and cons of, 103–104
 recognizing bargains on, 104–105
 service Websites, 106
Investment mortgages (*see* Mortgages)

Judicial foreclosure, 131

Kitchen fix–up costs, 183, 184

Land:
 lack of depreciation of, 204
 Land Contract of Sale, 132–133
Landlording, 7–8, 8, 149–175
 basic expenses and, 7, 32, 172
 businesslike approach to, 42–43,
  149–151
 children and, 143, 156
 cleanliness of property and, 78–79,
  145–146, 151–152
 conversion to rental and, 111–118
 eviction proceedings in, 158, 163,
  164–165, 181–182
 improving profitability in, 167–175
 and landlord/tenant laws, 151, 159
 and last month's rent, 157–159, 194
 late payments and, 160–161,
  162–164
 maintenance expense and, 7–8,
  32–33, 126, 172
 monitoring property in, 162
 pets and, 156, 157
 prompt attention to problems in,
  161–162
 raising rents, 161, 173–174
 renting for less than market value,
  159–160
 security/cleaning deposits and,
  158–159, 163, 194
 tenant analysis in, 30, 153–156
 utilities and, 144, 153, 172
 vacancy expense and, 7–8, 33, 114,
  126
 water bills and, 144, 153, 172
 (*See also* Tenants)

Landscaping:
 fix–up costs, 79, 143–144, 182
 water bills, 144, 153, 172
Last month's rent, 157–159, 194
Late payments:
 credit rating and, 124–125, 154–155
 of tenants, 160–161, 162–164
Lease–options, 191–201
 advantages of, 199
 components of, 193–195
 disadvantages of, 197–198, 200–201
 finding tenants for, 192–193
 qualifying tenants for, 198–199
 terms of, 194–198
Leases:
 breaking, 180–181
 last month's rent and, 157–159, 194
 in lease–options, 194
 sale of property and, 180–181
 security/cleaning deposits and,
  158–159, 163, 194
 term of, 169
 (*See also* Rental agreements)
Lenders:
 all–cash offers to, 80–81
 bad loans of (*see* Foreclosures;
  Government repos; REOs)
 for handyman specials, 100–101
 portfolio, 100–101
Leverage:
 annual return and, 5–6
 down payment and, 5–6, 44–45
 turnaround areas and, 66
Liability insurance, 32, 144–145
Lines of credit, 46
Liquidated damages clause, 19–20
Location of property, 28–29, 36–37,
  67–68, 79, 112, 220
Lot size, 143–144
Lowballing, 39–46
 avoiding attachment to property,
  42–43
 in beginning negotiations, 40
 cash reserves and, 45–46
 comparative market analysis (CMA)
  and, 40–41
 counter–offers in, 41, 42

Lowballing (*Cont.*)
  deciding amount of offer, 41
  down payment size and, 44–45
  elements of, 35–36
  of handyman specials, 98–100
  motivated sellers and, 51
LTV (loan to value) ratio, 113, 122, 218

Maintenance expense, 7–8, 32–33, 126, 172
Market price:
  CMA (Comparative Market Analysis) and, 34–35, 40–41
  defined, 11
  lease–options and, 196
  real estate recessions and, 4, 65
  renting under, 159–160
  turnaround areas and, 65–70
  (*See also* Lowballing)
MLS (Multiple Listing Service) and, 103, 185
Month–to–month rental agreements, 179, 180, 181
Mortgage insurance, FHA Section 203(k), 101
Mortgages, 121–128
  alienation clause in, 22, 130–132, 135
  assumable, 129, 133–135, 136
  in buying to convert, 127
  flipping and, 127–128
  manipulation of, 23, 85–86
  points and, 122–123
  preapproval of, 116–117, 199
  qualifying for, 122, 124–127
  refinancing, 7, 9, 113, 172, 216, 221–222
  second, 22–23, 133–135, 199
  (*See also* Down payment; Lenders)
Motivated sellers, 47–51
  of handyman specials, 99–100
  Internet listings and, 104, 107

Negative cash flow, 7–8, 167–175
Negotiations, lowball offers in, 40
Neighborhood analysis, 28–29, 79, 112, 140–141, 146, 220

Neighbors, as information source, 50–51
New developments, as turnaround areas, 68–69
Newspapers:
  conversion to rental and, 117–118
  local market analysis and, 30, 140–141, 146
  notice of default in, 56
Notice of default, 56

Offers:
  all–cash, 80–81
  for handyman specials, 98–100
  Internet listings and, 104
  for REOs, 79–81
  for repos, 87, 89, 91
  (*See also* Counter–offers; Lowballing)
Options (*see* Lease–options)
Owner–occupants:
  conversion to rental property (*see* Conversion to rental)
  income qualifying for mortgages, 125–127
  as landlords, 27
  repos and, 87–88, 92

Painting fix–up costs, 79, 183
Passive income, 209
Personal loans, 128
Pets, 156, 157
PITI (Principal, Interest, Taxes, and Insurance), 7, 32
Plaster fix–up costs, 79
Plumbing fix–up costs, 79, 141
Points, 122–123
Pool homes, 144–145, 153, 173
Portfolio income, 209, 211
Portfolio lenders, 100–101
Preapproval, 116–117, 199
Price/rent ratio, 30–31
Professional home inspection:
  for buyers of rental property, 188–189
  contingency for, 18–19, 99
  for handyman specials, 95

Professional home inspection (*Cont.*)
  for Internet listings, 104, 106
  for REOs, 82
  for repos, 88, 90, 91
Property managers:
  active income determination and,
    211
  number of properties owned and, 37
  recordkeeping and, 218
Property taxes, 7, 32
Purchase agreements, 61

Real estate agents/brokers:
  commissions of, 185, 186, 199
  double escrow and, 21–22, 50
  finding good, 185–186
  fix–up advice from, 184
  flipping by, 21–22, 50, 86
  foreclosures and, 55
  as investors, 49–50
  MLS (Multiple Listing Service) and,
    103, 185
  motivated sellers and, 49–50
  REO listings and, 76–77
  repo listings and, 87, 89, 90–91
  in selling a rental, 185–186
  Website listings of, 103, 104, 107–108
Real estate money tree, 217–223
Real estate options, 14–16
  (*See also* Lease–options)
Rebuyers:
  assignment and, 17, 21
  defined, 14
  flipping and, 12, 14
Recordkeeping, 215–216
Refinancing:
  in conversion to rental, 113
  ease of, 7, 9
  raising cash through, 221–222
  to reduce expenses, 172
  taxes and, 216
Rent discount, 161
Rental agreements:
  month–to–month, 179, 180, 181
  (*See also* Leases)
Rental properties, 139–147
  condition of, 141–142, 145–146

Rental properties (*Cont.*)
  conversion to (*see* Conversion to
    rental)
  economy and, 146–147
  lease–options and, 191–201
  location of, 139–141
  restrictions on, 112, 142–143
  type of, 141–145
REOs (Real Estate Owned), 71–84
  defined, 71
  finding, 75–77
  foreclosure and, 73–74
  making an offer for, 79–81
  pitfalls of, 82–84
  reasons for, 72–73
  refurbishing, 77–79
  secrecy behind, 74–75
  sources of, 71–72
  terms for, 81–82
Repair expense, 172
Repos (*see* Government repos)
Rescission of sales agreement, 62
Reserves, 45–46, 114, 115
Roof fix–up costs, 79, 96, 97, 141
Rule of 72, 228

Schools, 29
Screen fix–up costs, 79
Second mortgages, 22–23, 133–135,
  199
Security/cleaning deposits, 158–159,
  163, 194
Seller financing, 34, 44, 99–100,
  129–136
Selling, 179–203
  capital gains taxes and, 115–116,
    175, 208, 212–215
  closing the sale, 189–190
  disclosures and inspections in,
    188–189
  ease of, 8–9
  fix–up in, 182–185
  of handyman special, 101–102
  lease–options in, 191–201
  "by owner," 54–55, 103, 107–109,
    185, 186–189
  real estate brokers in, 185–186

Selling (*Cont.*)
  tenant removal in, 179–182
  (*See also* Flipping)
Sheriffs, 164
Single–family homes, 26, 90, 91, 112
Slab fix–up costs, 82–83
Small apartment buildings, as invest-
  ment properties, 27–28
Small Business Administration (SBA)
  repos, 92
Starker rule, 214
Swimming pools, 144–145, 153, 173

Tax–deferred exchange, 116, 213,
  214–215
Tax Reform Act of 1986, 206, 208
Taxes, 203–216
  capital gains, 115–116, 175, 208,
    211–215
  conversion to rental and, 115–116
  credits, 174
  depreciation and, 8, 115, 168,
    174–175, 203–211
  as infrequent expense, 170
  on lease–options, 199
  professional advice concerning, 175
  property, 7, 32
  record keeping and, 215–216
  reducing, 172
  refinancing and, 216
  savings from, 174–175
  tax basis and, 206–208, 215–216
  on tax–deferred exchanges, 116,
    213, 214–215
Taxpayer Relief Act of 1997, 208, 213
Tenants:
  children and, 143, 156
  converting to buyers, 191–201
  eviction proceedings and, 158, 163,
    164–165, 181–182
  lease–options and, 191–201

Tenants (*Cont.*)
  occupancy rate and, 26
  and owner–occupied buildings, 27
  pets and, 156, 157
  quality of, 8, 30, 153–156
  removing from rental property,
    179–182
  REOs and, 83–84
  strong tenant markets, 29–30,
    140–141
  tenant analysis, 30, 153–156
  utilities and, 144, 153, 172
  (*See also* Landlording)
Termite clearance, 187
Terms of deal, 33–34
Title insurance and trust companies:
  avoiding title, in flipping, 12, 131
  foreclosures and, 55–56, 60
  guaranteeing title, in foreclosure, 60
Townhomes, as repos, 90, 91
TransUnion, 124
Triplexes, as investment properties, 27
Trust deeds, foreclosure and, 55–56,
  131
Turnaround areas, 65–70

U.S. Army Corps of Engineers repos,
  92
U.S. Marshalls Service repos, 92
Utility bills, 144, 153, 172

Vacancy expense, 7–8, 33, 114, 126
Veteran Affairs Department repos, 92
Veteran's Administration (VA), 88–90,
  135

Walkway, front, 182
Wall board repair costs, 79
Water bills, 144, 153, 172
Websites (*see* Internet)
Window fix–up costs, 79

About the Author

Robert Irwin, one of America's leading experts in all areas of real estate, is the author of more than 40 books. His Tips and Traps series for McGraw–Hill has sold over a million copies. A broker and property investor as well as an advisor to consumers and agents, he has helped buyers and sellers solve their real estate problems for more than 20 years. He lives in Westlake Village, California. For more real estate tips and traps, go to www.robertirwin.com.